THE RIO GRANDE
SNIPER KILLINGS

THE RIO GRANDE
SNIPER KILLINGS

CAUGHT IN THE SIGHTS OF A DRUG CONSPIRACY

JOHN W. PRIMOMO

THE
History
PRESS

Published by The History Press
Charleston, SC
www.historypress.com

First published 2023

Manufactured in the United States

ISBN 9781467153430

Library of Congress Control Number: 2022949598

Notice: The information in this book is true and complete to the best of our knowledge. It is offered without guarantee on the part of the author or The History Press. The author and The History Press disclaim all liability in connection with the use of this book.

CONTENTS

ACKNOWLEDGEMENTS

Once again, the author is immensely indebted to Ms. Sandra Lynn Jesse for her many hours of careful and thoughtful editing. Her extensive literary experience has proven invaluable in ensuring that the story of Charlotte and Kevin did not become muddled by the author's legal discussions and explanations. Ms. Jesse's contribution to whatever success this book may enjoy was immense.

The author wishes to express special appreciation to Archie Carl Pierce, the federal prosecutor in the Rummel and Walker cases, who provided the trial transcript and other significant documents related to the Walker case. We met in person on two occasions and communicated numerous times via email. Carl provided his recollections and valuable insight into the Rummel and Walker cases and was always available to answer the author's questions at a moment's notice. John Murphy, Carl's co-counsel, likewise sat down with the author and made a significant contribution. Mike DeGeurin, Walker's defense attorney, graciously met with the author and freely gave his time and memories of Walker's representation. The author is also grateful to Tomas Tijerina, the owner of Pepe's, for his willingness to relive the terrible night of July 13, 1980, and to Richard "Dick" Braziel for his entertaining recollections of life as a DEA special agent and the case agent on the Loop 360 Deal.

Particular gratitude is expressed to Michael Wright of the National Archives and Records Administration (NARA) in Fort Worth and Adrianne Blake, an attorney on the compliance team within the Office of Information

Policy. Due to the pandemic, the NARA closed in 2020. Mr. Wright and his staff scanned nearly one thousand pages of a case file, which he provided to me electronically. Ms. Blake was instrumental in helping me obtain a response to an FOIA request, delayed for two years due to the pandemic. I am also thankful to Jo Lynn Trantham of the Hidalgo County Sheriff's Office, who copied numerous pages from the investigative records into the murder inquiry. She also diligently searched for photographs that might exist. Finally, I wish to thank Diana Garcia of the United States District Clerk's Office in San Antonio, who fielded many phone calls and greatly assisted the author in gaining access to court documents related to the case.

INTRODUCTION

It often happens that the real tragedies of life occur in such an inartistic manner that they hurt us by their crude violence, their absolute incoherence, their absurd want of meaning, their entire lack of style.
—Poet and playwright Oscar Wilde

In the summer of 1980, an amateur assassin hired to kill a federal grand jury witness fired a rifle into an open south Texas bar, missing his target and killing two young bystanders. Two innocent people died. Two families were devastated beyond words. On Sunday, July 13, 1980, Charlotte Kay Elliott, Kevin Edwin Frase and a host of Sunday pleasure-seekers chose to spend the afternoon and evening at Pepe's On the River, a popular outdoor recreation bar situated on the Rio Grande. By midnight, when Pepe's was closing, most of the crowd had gone home. Charlotte and Kevin were among thirty or so patrons who lingered. As they conversed with other customers and staff at the bar, a gunshot rang out from the parking lot, sending folks running for cover.

Everyone remained hidden until they were sure the shooter would not fire again. Frightened and cautious, the small crowd of patrons slowly emerged from their protection. As they scanned the area around the dance floor and bar, they were horrified by what they saw. Charlotte and Kevin lay on the floor, bleeding from head wounds; Charlotte was unconscious and dying, and Kevin was dead.

Charlotte and Kevin were not the hit man's targets. Tragically, they stood too close to the man the assassin intended to kill that night, a member of a drug conspiracy turned federal witness. Throughout this book, he shall be referred to only as Jimmy. For his privacy, his identity, even now, shall remain confidential. Jimmy was no saint, but he did not deserve to die.

In the fall of 1979, Jimmy joined a group of men planning to import four hundred pounds of marijuana into the United States from Mexico. As the pilot for the venture, he agreed to fly a small private plane carrying the marijuana from a remote landing strip in Mexico to Austin, Texas, where the drugs would be distributed. While Jimmy was still several miles south of Austin, air traffic controllers were alerted to a suspicious aircraft and began tracking his flight on radar.

After unloading the marijuana on a partially constructed highway in west Austin, Jimmy and another conspirator, John Christopher Burris, flew to the Austin airport, where they were met by federal drug agents and arrested. Austin police seized the marijuana. Jimmy and Burris were charged in federal court with marijuana trafficking. Federal prosecutors knew more people were involved. Jimmy and Burris could name the other participants, but they were not talking.

In the spring of 1980, after both men were convicted, they were summoned before a federal grand jury in Austin. Though they initially persisted in their refusal to cooperate, Jimmy and Burris relented when a federal judge held them in contempt. Anxious to be released from jail, they agreed to testify and identify their co-conspirators. Despite his promise, Burris assured his associates he would protect their identities, but no one knew what Jimmy would do. Several days before his grand jury appearance, the conspirators gathered in Jimmy's hometown of McAllen, Texas, to persuade him not to testify. Unable to secure his silence through bribery, talk turned to killing him. One of the accomplices, Boyce Wayne Rummel, hired an assassin, Lloyd Chris Walker.

On Sunday, July 13, the drug conspirators tracked Jimmy to Pepe's. Rummel drove Walker to the pub and pointed out Jimmy from the parking lot. Walker brazenly joined the crowd at Pepe's to get a close look at the man he intended to kill. Although the plan was for Walker to shoot Jimmy after he left, Walker and Rummel became increasingly impatient as the evening wore on.

Finally, near midnight, as Pepe's was closing, Jimmy and the remaining patrons and staff prepared to leave. Soon, the anxious killers, now sitting in Rummel's truck, would have their chance. Inexplicably, Walker decided he could wait no longer. He took a rifle, leaned out the passenger window, aimed at Jimmy as he stood in a group of people near the bar and fired. At the precise moment Walker took the shot, Charlotte, laughing, threw her head back, directly into the path of the bullet. It glanced off the back of her skull and split into two pieces; both fragments entered Kevin's neck, killing him almost instantly.

Jimmy survived the assassination attempt and immediately suspected who was behind the effort to kill him, but he did not know the hit man's identity. The investigation by law enforcement initially failed to turn up any leads. To his credit, Jimmy was not dissuaded from testifying before the grand jury. Based on his testimony, David Philip Ischy, another of the drug conspirators, was charged in federal court with drug smuggling. Ischy's criminal record included multiple drug arrests and a conviction, and he did not want to return to prison.

Ischy offered prosecutors valuable information in exchange for dismissal of the drug charge. He could name the person, Rummel, who hired the assassin. As part of his deal, Ischy even agreed to secretly record a conversation with Rummel, who unwittingly admitted to his role in the deaths of Charlotte and Kevin. Rummel's self-incriminating statements led to a state court indictment for capital murder.

Eventually, Rummel struck his own deal to avoid the death penalty. Willing to accept a forty-year federal prison term for intimidation of a federal witness, he agreed to identify and testify against Walker. Inexplicably, efforts to prosecute Walker in state court for capital murder proved unsuccessful. Federal prosecutors, determined that Walker should not go free, indicted him for attempting to kill a federal witness, Jimmy.

Walker's trial took place in federal court in San Antonio in June 1982 before United States district judge H.F. Garcia. As a young briefing attorney for Judge Garcia, the author sat through the trial, prepared the court's legal instructions and engaged in discussions with the lawyers on behalf of the court. The government was represented by a confident, aggressive prosecutor from the United States Attorney's Office, Archie Carl Pierce. Walker, though indigent, was defended by Mike DeGeurin, a reputable and experienced criminal defense attorney from Percy Foreman's law firm in Houston. Pierce was as determined to put Walker away for life as DeGeurin was to set him free.

At trial, Jimmy testified about his role in the drug deal and the attempt on his life. Eyewitness testimony about the murders also came from Pepe's owner Tomas Tijerina, whose acute observations and keen recollection of a customer who seemed out of place established that Walker was present at the murder scene on the night Charlotte and Kevin were killed. Rummel testified about his leadership role in both the drug and murder conspiracies and provided firsthand knowledge of the thoughts and actions of his associates.

Whether or not Walker would be convicted depended on who the jury believed—Rummel, who testified that he hired Walker and was sitting with him in the truck when Walker fired the rifle, or Walker, who denied he was the killer and claimed that Rummel was the shooter. DeGeurin skillfully cross-examined Rummel at trial, showing the jury why Rummel, motivated by self-preservation, would lie and implicate Walker. Pierce, too, realized a guilty verdict hinged on whether the jury believed that Rummel was telling the truth. Through evidence that corroborated Rummel's testimony and placed Walker at the scene, as well as pointed cross-examination of Walker and an exceptional closing argument, Pierce discredited Walker's testimony and gave the jury sufficient reason to convict him.

Rummel implicated not only himself but also other members of the drug deal in the murder conspiracy. Though guilty of marijuana trafficking, the remaining conspirators have never been charged with the murders of Charlotte and Kevin. They strongly denied any involvement in the decision to hire an assassin to kill Jimmy. Besides Rummel's testimony, no evidence exists to prove that the other men agreed to the assassination attempt. For the jury to find Walker guilty, they did not need to believe that anyone other than Rummel and Walker was part of the murder conspiracy.

Nothing in this book should be construed as suggesting that the other conspirators are guilty of or complicit in the murders of Charlotte and Kevin. Any reference to their involvement is based solely on the trial testimony of Rummel and has been included by the author to present the story as Rummel told it to the jury. The other members of the drug deal implicated during Walker's trial in the deaths of Charlotte and Kevin are presumed innocent of the murders.

Nevertheless, the other conspirators implicated by Rummel acknowledged participating in efforts to track Jimmy in McAllen and convince him not to testify. They also admitted knowing that Rummel hired an assassin to kill him. The tragedy of the deaths of Charlotte and Kevin is compounded by the fact that two of the drug conspirators faced, at most, no more than five years in prison if convicted, while the maximum sentence for Rummel and Ischy, who had prior drug convictions on their records, was ten years. Today, the same crime would carry a minimum of ten years and a maximum of life in prison. To avoid spending a few years in jail, shortened by the likelihood of release on parole, the decision was made to kill a human being.

The pain felt by the families of Charlotte and Kevin has not diminished in the four decades since they were murdered. The author was privileged to sit down with Kevin's brother, Keith, who shared precious memories of his beloved brother, and is immensely grateful to Kelly Chapman for her childhood recollections of her cousin Charlotte. Throughout the discussions of the drug and murder conspiracies, the court cases against Rummel and the prosecution of Walker, readers should never forget that the heart of this story is the devastating and unrelenting tragedy that shattered the lives of Charlotte, Kevin and their families.

Chapter 1

THE KILL SHOT

Driving along sparsely populated South Conway Avenue in Mission, Texas, a passerby might glimpse the remnants of a sign on a vacant lot that reads simply: "The River." Mission, located just west of McAllen, borders the Rio Grande, the narrow ribbon of water that forms the boundary between the United States and Mexico. Nothing on that vacant lot now resembles the festive scene that, for many years, enlivened the bar and dance hall known as Pepe's On the River. Opened in 1964 as Pepe's Boat Ramp by Jose "Pepe" de la Fuente, Pepe's operated as an outdoor recreation bar situated on the northern bank of the river.

Tomas Tijerina and his brother Luis bought the property from Pepe de la Fuente and then modified the original metal roof structure with a more attractive thatched covering. This *palapa* was relatively large, about fifty by one hundred feet, and open on all sides. Two mobile trailers were located adjacent to the main building in the parking lot, where tables and chairs accommodated any overflow crowd. Pepe's was described as part icehouse and part tropical paradise, owing to the palm trees surrounding the main structure. The popular drinking spot was slightly off the beaten path between the Rio Grande and a parallel levee on the U.S. side constructed to hold back floodwaters when the river became swollen from heavy rain. Proximity to the river subjected Pepe's to flooding whenever the waters of the Rio Grande rose. Consequently, some locals jokingly renamed the bar Pepe's *In* the River.

Pepe's On the River, circa 2006. *Courtesy of RV-Dreams.com.*

In 1980, Pepe's served crowds of regulars from the local population, who often brought friends and relatives from outside the Rio Grande Valley—"the Valley," as Texans refer to it—for the experience. And it was not exclusively frequented by folks on the U.S. side. At that time, the population of McAllen was approaching sixty-seven thousand, while directly across the border, the city of Reynosa, Tamaulipas, Mexico, boasted almost two hundred thousand inhabitants, providing an ample supply of Mexican patrons. Partygoers from both sides of the border could enjoy live music, dancing, barbecue, fried shrimp and other South Texas favorites with wine and pitchers of beer. Weekends were packed.

In addition to live entertainment, Pepe's featured a boat dock that offered customers the opportunity to ride jet skis on the river. The dock was also a convenient spot for drug smugglers to offload their marijuana and cocaine into the United States. Late at night, after Pepe's was closed, a speedboat might pull up to the ramp and, within seconds, unload its cargo of illegal drugs into a waiting truck or van. Both the boat and the loaded vehicle would then speed away.[1]

On Sunday afternoon, July 13, 1980, a local Kawasaki dealership brought its line of motorcycles and jet skis to exhibit for Pepe's customers. The Moses Rose Band provided live music from about seven o'clock to eleven thirty. A

Top: Photo of Pepe's from the levee. *Courtesy of Geoffrey Alger and the Mission Historical Museum.*

Bottom: Pepe's and the Rio Grande, circa 2008. *Courtesy of Pepe's on the River, via Facebook.*

local radio station even broadcast remotely from Pepe's, encouraging people to come out and enjoy the festivities. The crowd was immense. Tomas Tijerina estimated that between five and six hundred people were present. The cover charge was only a dollar to help pay for the band.

Among the crowd was eighteen-year-old Charlotte Kay Elliott. In May, Charlotte had graduated from Rolla High School in Rolla, Missouri, a town of about thirteen thousand located midway between St. Louis and Springfield on I-44, more famously known as Route 66. As a graduation gift, her parents paid for the trip to McAllen for Charlotte to visit her close friend Kathy Love, who had lived in Rolla before relocating. The girls frequented Pepe's several times in the weeks before July 13. The staff knew Charlotte by name. Now, near the end of her trip, Charlotte and Kathy returned one more time.

As is often the case with smaller communities like Rolla, a railroad bisects the town. The train runs due west for six hundred miles to Holcombe, Kansas, the site of another heartbreaking tragedy. In November 1959, Perry Smith and Dick Hickock murdered Herb Clutter (forty-eight), his wife, Bonnie (forty-five), and their teenage children, Nancy (sixteen) and Kenyon (fifteen), in their home, the subject of Truman Capote's bestseller *In Cold Blood*.

Charlotte Kay Elliott.
Courtesy of the Rolla High School Growler Yearbook.

In addition to her parents, Joe and Gloria Elliott, Charlotte's family included five siblings. Her dad worked hard. He owned a butcher shop in Rolla and hauled the mail from Rolla to St. Louis and Bourbon, Missouri. A U.S. Army veteran, Joe was a dedicated outdoorsman and was happiest in the saddle, carrying a fishing pole or hunting. Charlotte's mother was a talented musician and played the pipe organ at the local Lutheran church.

In the summer of 1980, Charlotte wore braces to enhance her constant smile and bubbly personality. Naturally blonde and blue-eyed, she stood five feet, six inches tall and weighed about 115 pounds. Charlotte personified a free spirit and was artistically gifted. Pictures she painted adorned the Elliott home. As a young teen, she enjoyed sharing stories as she curled her younger cousin's hair. The Elliott home was often the center of noisy family gatherings.

With high school behind her, Charlotte looked forward to the next big step in her young life. The independence of adulthood came with hopes, dreams and unlimited opportunities. Before planning her future, Charlotte intended to enjoy the summer, so in June 1980, she traveled to McAllen to visit Kathy. She intended to return home in a few weeks. On Sunday, July 13, Charlotte and Kathy arrived at Pepe's around four thirty in the afternoon.

Another Pepe's patron that day was a Valley native, twenty-eight-year-old Kevin Edwin Frase. Kevin was the oldest of three sons, and he and his brothers, Keith and Kirk, grew up in Donna, Texas, twelve miles east of McAllen. The boys' father, Rollin Frase, died in 1968 when Kevin was only a teenager, leaving their mother, Jane Vertrees Frase, to raise her three boys. Despite the hardship of working full time and raising her family as a single parent, she religiously attended every game and every school event in which her sons participated.

The Frase family. *Left to right*: Kevin, Keith, Jane Vertrees Frase and Kirk. *Courtesy of Keith Frase.*

Born March 18, 1952, the day after one of the men who orchestrated his death, Kevin worked at Edinburgh Hardware in 1980, selling and repairing guns. Following in his father's footsteps, Kevin learned the art of the gunsmith and became a ballistics expert. "Everyone took their guns to Kevin," recalled his brother Keith. Before working at Edinburgh Hardware, Kevin managed the gun department at Broadway Hardware in McAllen. In July 1980, he was residing with his mom and youngest brother, Kirk, in Donna; their middle brother, Keith, was married and living in Houston.

Kevin was handsome, lanky and six feet tall and weighed about 180 pounds. He had never married and had no children. Kevin was born with cerebral palsy, which causes abnormal reflexes, decreased muscle tone, rigidity of the limbs and trunk, abnormal posture, involuntary movements and an unsteady gait.[2] His right arm was severely affected, his right leg to a lesser extent. Kevin possessed a strong will, never felt sorry for himself and refused to allow his handicap to dictate how he lived his life. As a kid, he played football in the yard with his brothers. Kevin fearlessly engaged in any activity he wanted.

Kevin and Keith were very close and spoke weekly; they were brothers and best friends. Hunting with Keith was the best of life for Kevin. When Keith played football at Southwest Texas State University in San Marcos,

Keith's wedding. Kevin is in the first row in the center; Kirk is in the second row on the right. *Courtesy of Keith Frase.*

Kevin would finish work on Saturday at two o'clock in the afternoon and then drive five hours from Donna to San Marcos to attend the game. Keith recalled Kevin standing at the fence around the field, proudly watching his brother until Keith could break away from pregame warmups. Kevin enjoyed spending the night in the dorm with Keith after the game, giving the brothers valuable time to talk and share their lives.

Kevin was happy, endowed with a wry sense of humor, and he thoroughly enjoyed life. Anyone who knew Kevin would describe him as a good man who would do anything for anyone. He had no enemies, and no one would have wanted to hurt him.

From June throughout the summer of 1980, a massive heat wave in the United States wreaked havoc on the Midwest and Southern Plains. South Texas is always hot in the summer, and Sunday, July 13, was no exception; the thermometer hit 103 degrees.[3] Charlotte was accustomed to July temperatures in Rolla ranging from the mid-60s to the upper 80s, and the heat was stifling for her. Kevin grew up in South Texas and was more accustomed to the relentless Texas sun. Pepe's was an ideal respite for temporary relief from the soaring temperature. Customers could kick back, relax and enjoy the cool breeze blowing off the lazy, peaceful Rio Grande.

On Saturday, July 12, after finishing work at Edinburgh Hardware, Kevin began a welcome weeklong vacation. The next day, he and his friend Daniel Harris visited with friends before heading to Pepe's around five o'clock. Kevin was clean-shaven and wore a brown shirt, blue jeans, beige socks and brown loafers. Over the next several hours, Kevin and Daniel played pool and chatted with other customers.

As Tomas Tijerina prepared to close Pepe's around midnight, most customers had gone home; Monday was a workday. Perhaps thirty or more people remained. The band was breaking down its equipment, and Tijerina had released the security personnel. Recorded music continued to play to entertain the last few patrons. Charlotte was inside the main structure, sitting on a stool at the end of the bar. Kevin stood beside her, leaning on the bar because of his weak right leg. He was facing Charlotte, smiling and listening to what she was saying.

Standing within a few feet of Kevin and Charlotte was Jimmy, a regular Pepe's patron who knew many other customers. He lived in the McAllen area and had attended high school with Tomas Tijerina. He was even acquainted with Kevin from visits to Edinburgh Hardware. Jimmy was due to testify before a federal grand jury in Austin on Tuesday, July 15, about a failed marijuana importation scheme in which he had participated as the pilot. The conspiracy would later become known as the Loop 360 Deal, named for the unfinished highway in Austin where Jimmy landed the plane to unload the marijuana.

While the grand jury date was undoubtedly on his mind, Jimmy appeared as relaxed as everyone else. He knew his accomplices in the Loop 360 Deal did not want him to testify but was unaware they continued to stalk him. Desperate to prevent Jimmy from disclosing their identities, one of the men, Boyce Wayne Rummel, had hired a hit man, Lloyd Chris Walker, to kill him. As Jimmy played pool and socialized at Pepe's on July 13, 1980, Walker waited for his opportunity, going so far as to join the Pepe's crowd as a customer to get a close look at his target.

Walker was a ne'er-do-well from Austin. Born January 2, 1951, in Lawton, Oklahoma, to Lloyd and Jean Walker, he was known throughout his life as Mike. As a young man, Walker engaged in various delinquent activities just for the sake of excitement. On a dare, he broke into every café in Lawton—not to steal anything, just to prove he could do it. At eighteen, facing impending induction by the draft, Walker enlisted in the army and served a tour in Vietnam. Though he tried college and worked in various professions after leaving the army, his criminal tendencies ultimately directed his life. Walker boasted of skills as a "violent enforcer," so Rummel believed he was the man they needed.

Late in the afternoon of July 13, the drug conspirators tracked Jimmy to Pepe's. Rummel and Walker drove to the bar in Rummel's brown, two-toned pickup truck. From a vantage point in the parking lot, situated northwest of the palapa, Rummel pointed Jimmy out to Walker. Rummel remained in his truck, out of sight of Jimmy and the other Pepe's customers. After spending a couple of hours inside the bar, Walker walked back to the parking lot and told Rummel he had gotten a good look at Jimmy.

At Walker's trial, Rummel testified:

> Well, we were concerned there was a time limit on this, and since he might lose [Jimmy] again, well, then we probably would not be able to locate him before the next morning. And, so, we decided to wait there, and I believe—in fact, the plan was that we were going to wait there until sometime about ten o'clock that night and he had me bring the pickup truck—and a lot of people had left, and he had me move the pickup truck down to the closer parking lot.

As Rummel and Walker sat in the truck, they discussed the next move. Walker had no specific plan. Initially, he thought it would not be feasible to

A .30-.30 rifle with a scope. *Courtesy of Cheaper Than Dirt!*

shoot Jimmy at Pepe's; there were too many people. They decided to follow Jimmy when he left. As the night wore on, it became apparent Jimmy was staying at Pepe's for the long run. Rummel became more apprehensive—his mood and behavior aggravated by cocaine. At Walker's trial, David Ischy described Rummel's behavior as irrational and crazy, while Sonny Stotler said Rummel, at times, was no longer able to control himself. Dusk turned to darkness. By late evening, the crowd had thinned out considerably. Only about thirty people remained, customers and staff. The bar would be closing soon, and it was only a matter of time before Jimmy would walk directly to the parking lot. Rummel and Walker just needed to be patient a little longer.

Close to midnight, without explanation, Walker decided he could wait no more and told Rummel to start the truck. Walker retrieved Rummel's .30-30 rifle from under the seat and hung halfway out the passenger window. He looked through the scope, aimed carefully at Jimmy and fired. Not waiting to confirm his kill, Walker yelled at Rummel, "Let's go!"

After later visiting Pepe's, Keith Frase, an avid hunter, commented that he could not imagine how the assassin missed his target. Nothing was wrong with Walker's aim. At the moment Walker fired the rifle, Luis Tijerina, from behind the bar, said something funny to Charlotte. She threw her head back, laughing, just far enough to cross into the bullet's deadly path. But for that momentary, spontaneous reaction, Charlotte and Kevin would be alive and Jimmy would be dead. Tomas Tijerina saw her hair fly. The projectile grazed the back of her skull, knocking her off the stool. Her head smashed into the concrete floor. The glancing blow of the bullet off Charlotte's head did little to slow it down. It fractured into two pieces, both of which struck Kevin. No one heard either of them scream or cry in pain.

At Walker's trial, Tomas Tijerina testified about the tragic moment:

> *I heard what seemed to be an explosion or a loud bang, and I was standing behind the bar. One of my customers* [Charlotte], *who was sitting on the end, fell over off of a chair. And one of the guys* [Kevin] *was* [standing at] *the corner of the bar and fell backward.*

Tijerina knew Kevin from Broadway Hardware. Familiar with firearms from his service in the army, Tijerina was sure the sound he heard was a gunshot. He yelled for everyone to get down.

Tijerina further recalled:

> *All of the people at the bar took heed, and they were all on the ground, and I went around the bar down to the grassy area between the dock and the building, and I yelled at the musicians to get down because they had not heard anything.*

Before cell phones, calling the police and an ambulance meant using a landline on the wall or bar. Tijerina wisely hesitated before exposing himself or his staff in order to summon emergency assistance. After a couple of minutes passed without hearing another shot, Tijerina told an employee to call the Hidalgo County Sheriff's Office. Emergency personnel arrived within minutes.

Daniel Harris, who came to Pepe's with Kevin, recounted:

> *Well, around midnight, we heard a large crack underneath the shelter. And I went down because I was not sure if somebody was shooting somebody else, and I hit the floor, me and the person I was playing pool with. And, as I went down and looked around, I saw a* [blonde-headed] *girl fall in the bar area somewhere, so I was not sure what was going on.*

After about forty seconds, hearing no more noises, Daniel stood up and went to the bar. He saw Kevin lying on the ground, dead.

Kathy Love spent the evening both in and out of the thatched-roof building but was outside when she heard the shot. It sounded like a firecracker to Kathy, not as loud as it was to those under the main structure. She heard someone say a blonde woman went down. Kathy panicked and rushed inside; she saw Charlotte lying on the ground, unconscious. She became hysterical but then composed herself for her friend's sake. Kathy tried talking to and consoling Charlotte, but she never responded. Kathy stayed by her side until the ambulance arrived.

Because the Fourth of July had recently passed, Jimmy, Walker's intended target, thought the sound he heard was fireworks. He related the events inside Pepe's when the shot was fired and how very close he came to death:

Approximately quarter 'til twelve, I heard an explosion, and it sounded to me like a firecracker, and I could feel kind of fragments or felt like somebody had blown a firecracker up next to my hand. And I immediately saw a man that was standing next to me turn around, and he was falling with his face up to the ground with blood coming from the back of his head.

And I looked back to my left behind me—just back to here, and I saw a young blonde-headed woman also falling out of her chair backward with blood coming out of the back of her head.

I immediately ducked and ran.

A woman standing dangerously close to Jimmy was struck on the hand by a bullet fragment.

Jimmy had no idea where the shot came from. He sought shelter in a darkened area near the boat dock. After a short time, he heard a car speed away from the parking lot, squealing its tires on the caliche road. Assuming the shooter had left, Jimmy returned to the bar. He saw Kevin lying on the ground, bleeding profusely. He tried to render aid by giving mouth-to-mouth resuscitation, but it was no use.

Charlotte did not bleed a great deal, but Tijerina noticed a great deal of blood near Kevin. Nevertheless, he thought they both were still alive. Tijerina, Jimmy, Daniel and Kathy did what they could for Charlotte and Kevin until help arrived. They covered both victims and placed a blanket under Charlotte's head. Although both victims were unconscious, several people, including Jimmy, talked to Charlotte and Kevin in a futile effort to comfort them. Kevin died almost instantly; Charlotte died within two hours at a nearby hospital.

The Hidalgo County coroner performed an autopsy on each of the victims. According to the medical examiner, Charlotte and Kevin died of skull fractures and intracerebral hemorrhages. Charlotte's autopsy revealed that the bullet glanced off the back of her head, creating a three-and-three-quarter-inch laceration in her scalp. The medical examiner observed a pinpoint hole in her skull. He testified that the wound caused blood to accumulate within her skull, leading to compression of her brain and arteries and, eventually, death.

The bullet struck Charlotte with enough force to cause it to fragment. Part of the projectile entered the right side of Kevin's neck, penetrated the skin and lodged just under his right eye. A larger piece also entered the right side of Kevin's neck, moving upward until it passed out of his body between his eyes. The bullet fractured his jaw and the bone around his ear and fragmented his skull.

By the time the Hidalgo County Sheriff's Office deputies arrived at the scene, emergency personnel had transported Charlotte to the hospital. Tijerina directed the officers to the area near the bar where Kevin's body was covered by a sheet. In accordance with Texas law, the deputies summoned a justice of the peace to the scene. The judge pronounced Kevin dead at 1:04 a.m. Charlotte was pronounced dead at the hospital an hour later.

The deputies began an investigation, preserving the scene and speaking to witnesses. They searched Pepe's, including the parking lot, but found no weapon or spent rounds. No one at the scene could identify the shooter, though they said the shots appeared to come from the direction of the parking lot to the northwest. A witness stated she heard two vehicles depart the parking lot after the shot was fired. One witness recalled a brown, two-toned pickup truck.

The deputies re-created the incident by placing individuals in the positions of Charlotte and Kevin before the shooting. Even Jimmy participated, showing the deputies where he was standing. They made a rough sketch

Photo taken by investigators from the parking lot looking toward Pepe's, depicting the approximate direction of the kill shot. *Obtained via FOIA request from the United States Department of Justice.*

Another photo taken by investigators from the parking lot looking toward Pepe's, depicting the approximate direction of the kill shot. *Obtained via FOIA request from the United States Department of Justice.*

Photo taken by investigators from Pepe's looking toward the parking lot, depicting the approximate direction of the kill shot. *Obtained via FOIA request from the United States Department of Justice.*

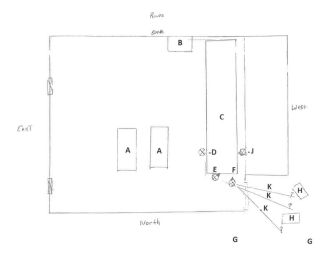

Sketch by Hidalgo County sheriff's deputies of the crime scene and the locations of Charlotte, Kevin and Jimmy. *Courtesy of the Hidalgo County Sheriff's Office.*

CRIME SCENE SKETCH LEGEND

A. Pool tables
B. Jukebox
C. Bar
D. Jimmy
E. Kevin Frase

F. Charlotte Elliott
G. Parking lot
H. Mobile trailers
J. Tomas Tijerina
K. Suspected directions of sniper fire

of the scene. Photographs of the reenactment were taken and later used as evidence at trial.

Deputies questioned Jimmy. Thinking back to an encounter on Friday night with one of the Loop 360 Deal conspirators, Jimmy did not take long to put two and two together. His grand jury appearance was only two days away, and an effort by his accomplices to buy him off had been unsuccessful. Jimmy now believed they were sufficiently desperate to prevent him from testifying that they had tried to kill him.

Jimmy told the investigating deputies the shot was meant for him. He said that he had recently been threatened "several" times because of his intent to testify, and he feared that the assassin would try again. The deputies asked if Jimmy knew anyone who lived locally that he suspected. He said no, but that "heavies" from Austin, including David Ischy, may have been behind the assassination attempt. The deputies also wanted to know if anyone else might be in danger. Another Loop 360 Deal conspirator, John Christopher Burris, was arrested with Jimmy in October 1979 and was also scheduled to testify before the grand jury. Jimmy told the deputies that Burris might be another potential target if he was not dead already. Jimmy had no idea Burris had helped Rummel track him down. After Jimmy assisted the deputies at the scene, a U.S. Customs officer, who knew he was a federal witness, escorted him home. Jimmy felt fortunate that he had survived the assassination attempt, but it hurt him deeply to know that two innocent people had died when he was the target.

At the scene, Tijerina was asked by the deputies if he had seen "anyone unusual or not part of the regular crowd." As the bar owner, he was attuned to his usual customers and those who were not regulars. With a keen recollection and auspicious perception, Tijerina recalled an individual who seemed out of place. He labeled the man as an "Austin type." Tijerina could show the deputies where he had been sitting—at a table near the trailers.

Tijerina described the "Austin-type" man as

> *a tall, slim fellow about twenty-five, twenty-seven. He had* [a] *long* [blonde] *ponytail, braided. He was wearing wire-rim gold frame glasses. He had a large set of muscles and was wearing a* [baseball] *cap that said Walker Company on it.*

The man also wore a cowboy shirt with pearl buttons. Tijerina described him "as a plain old Austin-type. And we don't have those down here." Not only could Tijerina describe the individual and point out where he had been sitting, but he also remembered what he was drinking: a Budweiser. Though Tijerina did not know his name, the man he identified was Lloyd Chris Walker.

The distressing and unenviable task of notifying next of kin remained. Being awakened in the middle of the night by a call or visit from someone in law enforcement is a parent's worst nightmare. Not wanting Joe and Gloria Elliott to receive the news from a stranger, Kathy Love courageously called Charlotte's sister in Rolla. Contemplating what Jane Frase and Joe and Gloria Elliott felt on that night when they received the news is painful, even now. The shock of hearing that your child is dead is indescribable, perhaps akin to being struck by an emotional lightning bolt.

The truth is unimaginable. You want it to be a nightmare, but it is not. Eventually, overwhelming and inconceivable emotional agony descended on Jane Frase and Joe and Gloria Elliott, a deep and powerful feeling that their hearts had been torn from their bodies.[4] Life as they knew it—the contented day-to-day living taken for granted when family is safe and secure—was gone forever. The Frase and Elliott families would never be the same. Jane Frase and Joe and Gloria Elliott could never be "normal" again. An emptiness existed that could never be filled. Just getting out of bed in the morning would require tremendous effort. Making it through the day became, at times, an overwhelming burden. Jane Frase knew that the clothes in Kevin's room would forever remain undisturbed. Joe and Gloria Elliott would never hear Charlotte's voice again or see her smiling face.

Certain days would be worse than others. July 14 would be a dreaded reminder for both families. For Jane Frase, March 18 would no longer be a joyful celebration of the day she gave birth to her first son but a reminder of the black hole in her heart. For Joe and Gloria Elliott, Charlotte's birthday, November 25, would be a painful anniversary. If they could bear to walk by Charlotte's artwork on the walls every day, maybe, over time, it would become a blessed memory of their daughter.

The fact that Charlotte and Kevin were murdered only made the pain worse. Parents always feel responsible for their children's safety. Now, Jane Frase and Joe and Gloria Elliott faced the disturbing reality that they had not protected Kevin and Charlotte. Devastated beyond comprehension by the unexpected loss of their children, they were forced to accept the brutal truth that Charlotte and Kevin would not be coming home. The inevitable question "Why did this happen to my child?" would flash through their thoughts but would never be answered.

Fortunately, Jane Frase was not alone. Kirk was with her, and her siblings were close. Somehow, she summoned the extraordinary strength to view Kevin's body at the mortuary. Keith remembered receiving the call in Houston around five o'clock in the morning on July 14 from his aunt, who delivered the tragic news with remarkable compassion and empathy. Keith and his wife then made the long and solemn drive to Donna. He could not bear to view Kevin's body; he needed to remember Kevin as he was in life. For Keith, the time in Donna after Kevin's death was a blur. Joe and Gloria Elliott had each other and their remaining children to help them cope with the terrible shock.

After completing their investigation at Pepe's, Hidalgo County deputies drove to the McAllen funeral home, where Charlotte's body had been taken from the hospital. At four thirty, Gloria Elliott called the undertaker. She provided deputies with Charlotte's full name and date of birth. Knowing that Charlotte had been shot in the head, Gloria asked that the autopsy not include other parts of her body. The coroner, who performed the autopsy later in the day after Charlotte's body was returned to the hospital, was aware that she had been shot. He needed to perform a complete autopsy to obtain evidence for the criminal investigation and determine precisely what factors contributed to Charlotte's death.

Chapter 2

THE LOOP 360 DEAL

T he genesis of the tragic murders of Charlotte and Kevin in July 1980 was a marijuana-smuggling operation conceived and unsuccessfully executed nine months earlier. The scheme would later become known as the Loop 360 Deal, named after the unfinished highway in Austin where Jimmy landed the plane carrying the load of marijuana from Mexico. As with most drug conspiracies, the object of the endeavor was simply to make money.

Indeed, the conspirators did not intend—initially, at least—that anyone would get hurt. They were blinded by the significant amount of fast and relatively easy money they would make importing marijuana into the United States and selling it to eager distributors. In the fall of 1979, as Charlotte began her senior year of high school in Rolla and Kevin lived and worked his young, contented life in Donna, no one could have imagined that a drug plot in which neither of them was involved would end their lives less than a year later.

Beginning in the early 1970s, the United States saw an unprecedented surge in the flow of illicit drugs. Despite the government's efforts to curb marijuana use, the demand for cannabis and other illegal drugs increased. Producers and importers enhanced their efforts to meet the growing demand. In 1979 alone, an estimated ten to fifteen thousand tons of marijuana were consumed in the United States.[5]

Initially, the primary federal agencies responsible for enforcing federal drug laws were the United States Customs Service and the Bureau of

Narcotics and Dangerous Drugs (BNDD). In 1973, Congress created the Drug Enforcement Administration (DEA) to focus and concentrate all federal drug efforts in President Nixon's declared "War on Drugs."[6] At the state level, the Texas Department of Public Safety (TDPS) was tasked with combatting the smuggling of illegal drugs.

In the late 1970s, Robert Nesteroff, a drug investigator with the TDPS, worked closely with Richard "Dick" Braziel of the DEA in investigating the importation of illegal drugs into the United States through Texas. Much of their work involved investigations within the Western District of Texas, one of ninety-four federal judicial districts and three territorial courts in Guam, the Northern Mariana Islands and the Virgin Islands. Geographically, the Western District of Texas is one of the largest federal districts, extending from El Paso, Midland and Del Rio in the west to San Antonio in the east, then north through Austin to Waco. The sheer size of the Western District and its proximity to the border with Mexico make it perhaps the most challenging federal district in the United States for law enforcement. The Loop 360 Deal was precisely the type of drug-smuggling operation Braziel and Nesteroff hoped to catch.

Investigative techniques took many forms. Braziel and Nesteroff regularly visited fixed-base operations (FBOs) at Central Texas airports. An FBO is a private organization granted the right by an airport to provide aeronautical services such as fueling, hangaring, tie-down and parking, aircraft rental, aircraft maintenance, flight instruction and similar services. By checking with the FBOs to obtain information about planes flying to and through Central Texas airports, Braziel and Nesteroff received vital information regarding suspicious aircraft. If they had reason to believe that an aircraft was being or would be used to transport illegal drugs, they could seek a search warrant or court authorization to place a transponder on the plane to track its movements. Once Braziel and Nesteroff began an investigation, they coordinated with an assistant United States attorney (AUSA), responsible for prosecuting federal crimes. Search and arrest warrants required court approval. Before presentation to a court, AUSAs review the requests to ensure the facts meet the legal standard for a warrant.

In the late '70s, two AUSAs for the Western District of Texas responsible for prosecuting federal drug crimes were Archie Carl Pierce and John Murphy. Pierce and Murphy, young AUSAs at the time, were members of the Controlled Substance Unit. In addition to assisting each other on their assigned cases, they played a prominent role in coordinating efforts between state and federal law enforcement agencies investigating drug crimes in the Western District. Knowing that information obtained by state law enforcement could be vital in his federal prosecutions, Pierce opened communication channels directly with the TDPS and local police.

Pierce worked closely with Braziel, whom he compared to Hank Schrader, the DEA agent in the television series *Breaking Bad*. Schrader was extroverted, fearless and eager to take on dangerous investigations. Talking to Braziel about his years in drug enforcement, the similarities with Schrader are plain to see. Retired now, Braziel remains as active and energetic as when he chased drug smugglers through Texas.

Laid-back and speaking with a comforting Texas drawl, Braziel related how he began his career in law enforcement as a police officer for the City of Fort Worth. He then joined the Customs Service to conduct narcotics investigations on the Texas-Mexico border between 1970 and 1974. Ironically, the murders of Charlotte and Kevin were not the first time Braziel heard of Pepe's On the River. He recalled eating barbecue and drinking beer at Pepe's during his tenure on the border.

In 1973, Braziel turned in his Customs badge and became a DEA special agent. A year later, he was transferred to the Lubbock, Texas drug task force, where he worked undercover "buying dope." After seizing an airplane with a large load of marijuana, Braziel spent two years deep undercover with airplane smugglers all over Texas. Though it is perhaps a DEA agent's most dangerous duty, Braziel recalled that working undercover could be fun. As part of his DEA duties, Braziel sometimes traveled to foreign countries to return U.S. criminals arrested outside the country who, as Braziel put it, had "fugitated" from justice. He was the DEA's designated case agent for the Loop 360 Deal.

For marijuana smugglers—like the Loop 360 Deal conspirators—the late 1970s and early 1980s were considered the "glory days." The illegal trade was risky but paid significant dividends. Recalling his first two nights of drug smuggling, one former smuggler said, "It was the greatest thing in the world. Here I am, just 21 years old; I got ten grand in my pocket." The rewards went up from there. "It was fun [and] exciting," said another smuggler, "a lot of adrenaline. Running around in the middle of the night, beating the Man at it. It was almost a game."[7]

Usually, smuggling drugs into the United States was accomplished without the intent or need to resort to violence.[8] "We weren't violent by any stretch of the imagination," said a former smuggler. "We were just a bunch of good ol' boys. We ran around with no shoes on, cut-off jeans, having a good time just like other kids in their early to mid-20s—but we had this thing going on, this opportunity to make killer money because we all, you know, smoked it, grew up with it."[9]

In the 1970s, most marijuana that came through South Texas from Mexico was warehoused in Austin after importation. "Cooler" than Dallas or Houston and more entertaining than the Rio Grande Valley towns, Austin was a favorite spot for wholesalers and brokers to gather and check out the quality of the cannabis. High-quality marijuana was cheap and abundant in Austin. The University of Texas at Austin, with its student population of over forty thousand in each academic year of the 1970s, provided an ample consumer base. College kids did not care what the stuff looked like or what it was called; they just wanted it to get them high.[10]

The Loop 360 Deal exhibited all the hallmarks of a typical South Texas marijuana-smuggling operation. The smugglers ranged in age from their mid- to late twenties, eager to make a great deal of money for minimal work. Their plan was simple. The marijuana would be bought cheaply in Mexico and flown directly to Austin in a private plane. The load of approximately four hundred pounds of marijuana was expected to sell for about $80,000 in the United States. Each conspirator would receive a share of the profits, depending on his role in the conspiracy. The organizers and the pilot received the most; accomplices who merely loaded and unloaded the marijuana received a much smaller share.

The Loop 360 Deal was orchestrated by Boyce Wayne Rummel and David Phillip Ischy. Rummel and Ischy, who met in prison in the mid-1970s, were well known to Braziel, Nesteroff and other law enforcement agents in South and Central Texas because of their propensity to engage in drug smuggling. According to Braziel, Rummel and Ischy ran with a group of marijuana smugglers, including Austin attorney John Webster Flanagan and his sons.[11] Beginning in 1979, according to Rummel, he and Ischy engaged in various drug deals together.

By 1979, when they organized the Loop 360 Deal, the criminal records of both Rummel and Ischy included convictions in federal court for drug offenses. In 1975, a year or so after his college graduation, Rummel, age twenty-three, was convicted of conspiracy to import almost one thousand pounds of marijuana from Mexico. He spent a little more than eleven months in federal prison. Incarceration did little to deter him from reengaging in criminal activity. His co-defendant in that case, William Clayton "Sonny" Stotler, teamed up with Rummel again for the Loop 360 Deal.

David Ischy proved to be a prolific drug dealer throughout most of his life. In December 1972, he was indicted in federal court for possession of more than 470 pounds of marijuana with the intent to distribute. He pleaded guilty to the charge and, in 1974, was given five years' probation, which required him to comply with several conditions, including the critical requirement that he refrain from further violations of the law. In 1978, while on probation, he was charged again in federal court with conspiracy to import marijuana and marijuana importation. Pending a hearing on a motion to revoke his probation, Ischy was granted a bond on November 8, 1978. Like probation, release on bond required that Ischy not violate the law. In November 1979, while on bond and probation, Ischy was arrested for possession of marijuana.

In the fall of 1979, Ischy approached Rummel and proposed importing a load of marijuana from Mexico into the United States. Ischy already had the financier who would supply the money to buy the marijuana and pay other expenses. Rummel readily agreed to the proposal. His Mexican connections and prior experience with marijuana-smuggling activities allowed him to pull it off. Eventually, this transaction became known as the Loop 360 Deal.

A U.S. operator like Rummel often relied on Mexican contacts to bring the marijuana north, at least as far as Mexico City or Monterrey. A South Texas Hispanic or a northern Mexican related to someone in a Texas border town would transport the load to a point where it could be imported into the United States. Rummel's brother-in-law and co-conspirator, Richard Servantez, had ties to Mexico.

Born and raised in San Antonio, Rummel graduated from Southwest Texas State University in San Marcos, thirty miles south of Austin, with a degree in sociology and psychology. By his admission, his involvement with drugs began in college. In addition to marijuana, Rummel dabbled in cocaine and methamphetamine for personal use, especially in 1980. In 1979 and 1980, he was using cocaine regularly. When not dealing drugs, Rummel operated an antique sales and restoration business.

After Rummel and Ischy agreed to the deal, Rummel sought out other people they would need. The name of the primary financier Ischy brought to the conspiracy was never disclosed. During the trial of Charlotte and Kevin's killer, the unnamed financier was alluded to as someone willing to kill to avoid being identified. Other Loop 360 Deal conspiracy members included Stotler, Servantez, John Christopher Burris and George Crisp. Rummel also needed a pilot.

Burris met Rummel in the early '70s and was renting a house from him in the fall of 1979. He told Rummel he knew someone who could fly the marijuana from Mexico into the United States. Burris and Jimmy had known each other since childhood; even Ischy had met Jimmy. At Walker's trial, Jimmy represented that the Loop 360 Deal was the only illegal scheme in which he had ever participated.

Rummel testified that he understood differently:

> PIERCE: *Did you know at the time—did you know Jimmy? By reputation or otherwise?*
>
> RUMMEL: *By reputation, yes.*
>
> PIERCE: *And you knew he was a pilot for drug activities?*
>
> RUMMEL: *All kinds of activities.*
>
> PIERCE: *What other activities?*
>
> RUMMEL: *Drugs, guns, electronic equipment, flying in and out of Mexico, basically. Contraband.*
>
> PIERCE: *It was known before you set up this 360 transaction that he [had] quite extensive experience in smuggling contraband in and out of Mexico?*
>
> RUMMEL: *Yes.*

Jimmy grew up in McAllen. In the fall of 1979, he was twenty-six years old. Like Rummel, Jimmy was college-educated; he spent two years at Pan American University in Edinburg, Texas. Jimmy's role as the aviator would earn him a great deal of money for little work. In exchange for renting a plane, flying to Mexico to pick up the load and then flying the marijuana from Mexico to Austin, Jimmy would be paid the considerable sum of $15,000—over $50,000 in today's economy.

Needing to avoid airports and landing strips where he might be seen, Jimmy planned to land at a makeshift airstrip on Loop 360 in west Austin, which was then under construction. In addition to his connection to the financier, Ischy, with Crisp's help, was responsible for "landing" the plane. They arranged for people to unload the marijuana and a vehicle to transport the load. They drove to the designated location on Loop 360, set up lights to illuminate the road for a night landing and met Jimmy when he touched down.

Before flying to Mexico, Jimmy removed four of the six seats from the airplane to make more room for the marijuana. The seats were loaded into a truck in McAllen, which Stotler then drove to the landing site in Austin. Servantez drove to the Mexican landing site with Rummel. He helped load the marijuana in Mexico and acted as an interpreter for Rummel with the Mexican supplier.

Rummel anticipated the venture would be quite profitable. He paid a Mexican national 1,300 pesos ($56) per kilo for the four hundred pounds of marijuana—roughly $10,000. Rummel expected the marijuana would bring $200 a pound in the United States. Servantez, Stotler and Crisp would be paid a flat fee of $2,500 each. After paying Jimmy $15,000, Rummel, Ischy and Burris would receive one-third of the net profits, which Rummel estimated to be $20,000–$25,000 each.

On October 9, 1979, Jimmy chartered a single-engine Cessna 206 from McCreery Aviation in McAllen. On the rental invoice, he indicated he would fly the plane to Dallas with a stop in Austin. Of course, nothing was mentioned about Mexico or marijuana. After removing the seats, he flew with Burris to Mexico on October 10, 1979. At Walker's trial, Rummel testified regarding his part in the deal:

> *I arranged the schedule with David Ischy and Chris Burris as to when to come down and get the marijuana, and once I was down there, I arranged for a strip down there, and obtained the marijuana and moved it to the landing strip.*

The landing site was near Tula, Tamaulipas, Mexico, approximately three hundred miles south of the border, between Monterrey and San Luis Potosí. Known as the Governor's Strip, the runway, which belonged to the Mexican military, was about four thousand feet long and unpaved. In addition to the cash, Rummel provided a couple of shotguns and several boxes of shells to the drug supplier as part of the purchase price. The marijuana was packed into fifty-four sacks, some burlap and some plastic. All but one sack was loaded into the plane; there was no more room. After the plane refueled and took off, Rummel and Servantez drove back to the United States.

Jimmy and Burris flew first to a deserted airstrip in Falfurrias, Texas, eighty miles north of the border, where they stopped only long enough to place green adhesive tape over the wing lights. From there, they flew directly to west Austin and landed shortly after midnight on the partially completed Loop 360, south of what is now the Pennybacker Bridge spanning the Colorado River. Jimmy kept the plane running; he did not want to be on the ground long. With the help of Ischy, Crisp and other unnamed individuals, the marijuana was unloaded into the camper of Burris's white pickup truck. The seats removed to make room for the marijuana were thrown back into the plane. Then, Jimmy and Burris took off and flew the short distance to Ragsdale East FBO at the Robert Mueller Airport on Austin's east side. The worst part was over, or so they thought.

Aerial photo of Jimmy's landing site on Loop 360.
Court records in National Archives and Records Administration, Fort Worth, Texas.

Often, the discovery of a crime is attributable to pure luck—good luck for law enforcement, bad luck for the criminals. The nighttime flight of Jimmy and Burris from Mexico had not gone unnoticed. A jogger in Falfurrias watched as the marijuana-laden plane landed and one of its occupants nefariously covered its navigation lights with tape. Law enforcement authorities were notified, and Houston air traffic control (ATC) began tracking the unlit aircraft on radar.

Aware of clandestine efforts by drug smugglers to fly marijuana into the United States, the ATC dispatcher notified a United States Customs agent in San Antonio about the suspicious flight. The agent rushed to Kelly Air Force Base, boarded a Customs plane and flew to Jimmy's last known location near Lockhart, twenty miles south of Austin. Throughout his pursuit, the Customs agent remained in contact with Houston ATC, which guided him toward Jimmy's plane.

Near Austin, the Customs plane was handed over to Austin ATC, which began tracking Jimmy's aircraft. The FBO at Mueller Airport contacted Robert Nesteroff of the TDPS about the suspicious plane. Austin ATC observed Jimmy, west of Austin, circle several times and then disappear from radar. The Customs agent was directed to Jimmy's last radar sighting and soon located the landing site on Loop 360. Despite the darkness, and probably thanks to the landing lights set up by Ischy and Crisp, the Customs agent found the plane and noticed several vehicles close by.

After Jimmy and Burris took off, they flew the short distance to Mueller Airport, where, unknown to the two smugglers, law enforcement officers were waiting. Shortly after midnight on October 11, Jimmy and Burris were detained, and the aircraft was searched. Officers found that the seats had been haphazardly tossed into the back, a common indicator that the plane had been used to transport drugs. Agents also found marijuana debris on the floor. Inside the aircraft was a map of South Texas and northern Mexico with a line drawn from McAllen to Tula, Jimmy's initial direction of travel. They noticed that the navigation lights had been taped over, an obvious sign that Jimmy did not want to be detected. Everything pointed to a marijuana-smuggling operation.

 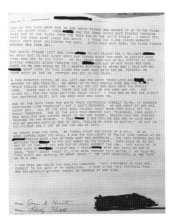

Left: Statement of a witness to the unloading of the marijuana on Loop 360 from Jimmy's plane (part 1). *Court records in National Archives and Records Administration, Fort Worth, Texas.*

Right: Statement of a witness to the unloading of the marijuana on Loop 360 from Jimmy's plane (part 2). *Court records in National Archives and Records Administration, Fort Worth, Texas.*

Taped navigation light on Jimmy's plane. *Court records in National Archives and Records Administration, Fort Worth, Texas.*

Meanwhile, the Customs plane tracked the white pickup truck loaded with marijuana and notified Austin police. From his vantage point in the air, the Customs agent directed the police vehicles, which he could identify by their emergency lights, toward the load vehicle. Ironically, the name of the Austin police officer with whom the Customs agent maintained contact was Chris Walker. By the time police caught up to the load vehicle, it had been driven to a mobile home in West Austin, where the marijuana was seized.

Police uncovered additional marijuana inside the mobile home and arrested the occupant. Both Crisp and Ischy were gone. Stotler had observed the surveillance plane over the landing site and warned Ischy that he and Crisp should leave. Austin police stopped two vehicles as they departed from the mobile home. From questioning the occupants, police gathered more information about the conspiracy, including David Ischy's involvement. Nesteroff, who coordinated efforts on the ground, called Braziel about the seizure of the marijuana and the plane and the arrests of Jimmy and Burris; Braziel then called AUSA Pierce.

Later that day, October 11, Ischy appeared at Rummel's house. He told Rummel the marijuana had been seized and that Jimmy and Burris had been arrested. Ischy and Rummel immediately became concerned that Jimmy and Burris might cooperate with law enforcement authorities and identify other members of the drug conspiracy. Ischy was particularly nervous, knowing that another conviction on top of his multiple prior felony drug cases would almost certainly result in substantial prison time. Rummel had known Burris a long time and believed it was unlikely he would snitch on them. They could not be so sure about Jimmy.

After their arrest, Jimmy and Burris were charged in state court in Austin with conspiracy to engage in organized crime. Coordination between state and federal prosecutors led to the dismissal of the state charge and their indictment in federal court for possession and importation of marijuana. Jimmy and Burris could have been prosecuted for the drug crime at both the state and federal levels. But as a practical matter, a person will be charged in either state or federal court, not both.

The factors in this situation weighed in favor of federal prosecution. Jimmy's plane was initially pursued by a U.S. Customs agent, and the map found in the aircraft suggested that the drugs were imported. Federal criminal charges are usually filed when a large quantity of drugs is seized or when the scheme involves a conspiracy among a large group of people. The four hundred pounds of marijuana seized was substantial. Based on the observations of the Customs agent who flew over the Loop 360 landing site

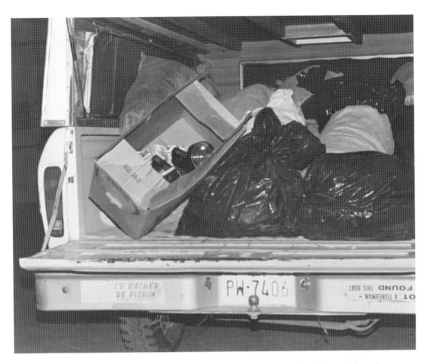

White camper loaded with marijuana. *Court records in National Archives and Records Administration, Fort Worth, Texas.*

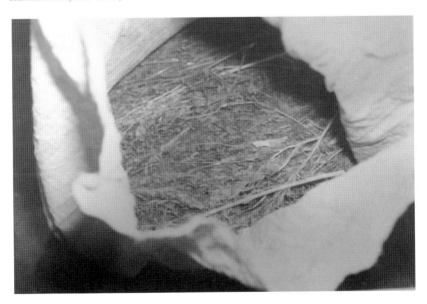

Bag of marijuana seized by Austin police on October 11, 1979. *Court records in National Archives and Records Administration, Fort Worth, Texas.*

and the questioning of suspects by Austin police, law enforcement was also aware several other individuals were involved. The decision was made to turn the case over to the United States Attorney's Office for prosecution in federal court in the Western District of Texas.

Prosecution of the Loop 360 Deal was assigned to Pierce, who presented the case to a federal grand jury in San Antonio in November 1979. In addition to Jimmy, Burris and Ischy, James Cecil Flanagan, Royce Reynolds and Joy Ann Tabor were named in the original indictment. Crisp was later added as a defendant. At that time, law enforcement authorities were unaware of Rummel, Stotler and Servantez.

Based on the information received by law enforcement, Pierce believed that Flanagan and Reynolds helped Ischy and Burris unload the marijuana at the Loop 360 landing site. Tabor occupied the mobile home where the marijuana was seized. Each was charged with conspiracy (the agreement) to possess with intent to distribute marijuana, possession with intent to distribute four hundred pounds of marijuana, conspiracy to import marijuana and importation of four hundred pounds of marijuana. In most conspiracies, the prosecution relies on the testimony of one or more conspirators against the others. For the original Loop 360 Deal indictment, information was obtained not from a conspirator but from a person who claimed to have been present at the Loop 360 landing site and to know about the participants. That person's testimony led to the indictment of Ischy, Crisp, Flanagan and Reynolds. Unfortunately for Pierce, when questioned during a pretrial hearing, the informant proved unreliable. The person could not identify Flanagan and Crisp and was confused about the other alleged conspirators and the events surrounding the seizure of the marijuana.

Without credible testimony, sufficient proof was lacking to prosecute Ischy and the others. Rather than risk the possibility that Ischy would be acquitted and be protected from further prosecution for the Loop 360 Deal by the double jeopardy clause, Pierce dismissed the indictment against everyone except Jimmy and Burris. He still had a solid case against them.

Jimmy and Burris had two options. They could go to trial on the indictment or accept a plea bargain and plead guilty to one or perhaps two of the four charges. If they pleaded guilty, they most likely would receive a lighter sentence, maybe even probation. But as part of a plea agreement, the government would require Jimmy and Burris to debrief with DEA special agent Braziel about the Loop 360 Deal and implicate the other conspirators. Neither man was willing to do that. Despite substantial evidence of their guilt, they went to trial in San Antonio in February 1980.

Jimmy and Burris waived their right to a jury and agreed that United States district judge D.W. Suttle could decide their guilt or innocence. The evidence was more than sufficient. Jimmy and Burris were convicted of conspiracy and possession of the marijuana with the intent to distribute. They were, however, acquitted of the counts of the indictment related to importation. Judge Suttle found that, despite the circumstantial evidence linking the plane to Mexico, there was no direct proof that the marijuana had been imported, only that it was seized in Austin.

As punishment for their parts in the Loop 360 Deal, Jimmy and Burris were sentenced in April 1980 to serve terms of four years of confinement in the custody of the Federal Bureau of Prisons. Because Jimmy was convicted of a drug offense, the Federal Aviation Administration suspended his pilot certification. Things got exponentially worse for him after that.

Chapter 3

THE HUNT

Pierce knew Jimmy and Burris were his only link to the other Loop 360 Deal conspirators. The testimony from the informant who claimed to be at the Loop 360 landing site proved useless, and none of the physical evidence seized from the airplane incriminated anyone else. If they would not voluntarily provide the details about the conspiracy and the other people's identities, Pierce would compel them to testify. In May 1980, shortly after Jimmy and Burris were sentenced, he summoned them before a federal grand jury in Austin.

As expected, Jimmy and Burris declined to appear. Ordinarily, an individual's refusal to testify is based on the Fifth Amendment to the United States Constitution, which provides that no person "shall be compelled in any criminal case to be a witness against himself," better known as the right to remain silent. Although the government could not force Jimmy and Burris to incriminate themselves, that was not what Pierce was trying to do. He did not intend to use Jimmy and Burris's testimony as evidence *against them*; they had already been convicted. Instead, Pierce sought the information to identify and prosecute other conspiracy members.

Once Jimmy and Burris were convicted and sentenced, the Fifth Amendment privilege no longer protected them from providing information about their roles in the Loop 360 Deal. Also, Pierce granted both men testimonial immunity, which meant their grand jury testimony could not be used to prosecute them for other criminal activity that might be discovered because they were compelled to testify. Unwilling though they may be, they had no legal basis for refusing to testify before the grand jury.

Of course, Jimmy and Burris probably had other reasons for not wanting to implicate Rummel, Ischy and the others. When it comes to words with a negative connotation, the term *snitch* is probably near the top. Prosecutors prefer to use less offensive expressions like *informant* or *cooperating witness*. If the snitch label follows a defendant to prison, he may face the wrath of other inmates, some of whom ended up in jail because of information provided to law enforcement by one of their criminal accomplices. Generally, snitches are treated as outcasts in prison—extorted, bullied, physically/sexually assaulted and even murdered.

Besides not wanting to be disloyal to their partners in crime, Jimmy and Burris may have feared for their safety if they identified the other Loop 360 Deal participants, a fear that proved to be fully justified. However, the constitutional right to remain silent applies only to *self*-incrimination; in other words, a person cannot be forced to say something that could be used as evidence against him in his criminal trial. The Fifth Amendment does not shield a defendant from testifying against someone else. A defendant cannot refuse to testify if the sole basis for his refusal is the possibility that doing so might place his life or even the life of a loved one in danger.

When Jimmy and Burris failed to appear before the grand jury, Pierce took the next legal step by requesting that a United States district judge order them to comply with the summons and testify. At a hearing, they were provided the opportunity to assert any legal defense to the grand jury summons. They had none. The judge ordered Jimmy and Burris to appear and answer Pierce's questions. At that point, they could either choose to obey the order or risk being held in contempt of court. Initially, both men persisted in their refusal.

Despite Hollywood portrayals of court proceedings where judges threaten and impose contempt regularly, courts do not take the sanction lightly or use it often. Holding a person in contempt is sometimes necessary to enforce court orders and maintain judicial integrity. In the context of a refusal to obey an order to testify in court or before a grand jury, contempt usually means incarceration until the individual agrees to testify. Although a person could be jailed almost indefinitely, being locked up generally produces the desired effect of loosening the person's tongue.

A second hearing was held to determine if Jimmy and Burris should be held in contempt of court, but the result was a foregone conclusion. They had not complied with the order requiring them to testify; nothing else mattered. The judge held them in contempt and remanded them to jail. Both men had been released on bond pending the appeals of their convictions.

The contempt order put them back in jail. They would remain there until they "purged" themselves of contempt by appearing before the grand jury and answering Pierce's questions about the Loop 360 Deal. And as their attorneys undoubtedly told them, the time served while in contempt did not count toward the sentences they received. As long as they were incarcerated under the contempt order, their drug sentences were, in effect, suspended.

After sitting in jail for several weeks, they relented. Jimmy and Burris told Pierce they would cooperate, appear before the grand jury and testify to their knowledge of the facts and participants in the Loop 360 Deal. Because of their change of heart and relying on their promise to testify, Pierce agreed they could be released until the grand jury convened on Tuesday, July 15, 1980. Jimmy traveled back to McAllen, his hometown.

From the beginning of the prosecution of Jimmy and Burris in late 1979, Ischy and Rummel followed the proceedings closely. They spoke regularly, worried that Jimmy or Burris might decide to cooperate with the government and implicate the other members of the Loop 360 Deal. More significantly, the person who financed the drug conspiracy—the person at the top of the criminal enterprise, whom Pierce wanted most of all—made it unmistakably clear he must not be identified; if he were, there would be consequences.

Beginning in February 1980, after Jimmy and Burris were convicted, and continuing into May 1980, when they were held in contempt of court, Ischy and Rummel's concern intensified. Burris, who had known Rummel since 1970, assured his friend that he would not testify, despite what he told Pierce. Burris did not specify whether he would "fugitate" or testify and simply muddle the facts. Perhaps he intended to feign lack of knowledge or loss of memory to avoid implicating Rummel, Ischy and the others.

Jimmy was another matter. Rummel had only known him since the inception of the Loop 360 Deal in the fall of 1979—Ischy, not much longer. Though Burris had been acquainted with Jimmy since childhood, he did not know Jimmy well enough to assure Rummel and Ischy that he, too, could be trusted. As time passed and the grand jury appearance grew closer, the topic of conversations between Rummel and Ischy evolved from whether or not Jimmy would cooperate with law enforcement to what they could do to prevent it. Ischy told Rummel that he, Rummel, was responsible for the problem because he brought Jimmy into the transaction. In no uncertain terms, speaking for himself and the unnamed financier, Ischy warned Rummel that he had more to worry about than being implicated in a drug conspiracy.

Rummel believed the person who backed the venture was a "large scale operator." At Walker's trial, Rummel testified:

> *Anyway, David Ischy implied to me that was the situation concerning the people that provided the money through him. And, if certain steps weren't taken to prevent—to prevent David Ischy's involvement, or their involvement, then I would have things to worry about.*

Rummel understood what that meant: his own life would be in danger.

Relying on Burris's assurance that he would remain discreet, Rummel and Ischy focused on what they should do about Jimmy. Perhaps he would agree not to testify in exchange for a monetary bribe; that was the first option. If he could not be persuaded, killing him had to be considered.

Rummel and Ischy had been young marijuana traffickers with little respect for the law, but their willingness to take a human life elevated them to a far more sinister criminal category. Neither Rummel nor Ischy had committed a violent crime in the past. Now, the thought of going back to jail and the fear of reprisal by the financier led them to shutter their conscience and ignore their morality. If the only way to stop Jimmy from testifying was to kill him, that is what they would do.[12]

At Walker's trial, Rummel testified that he and Ischy were not the only Loop 360 Deal conspirators aware that it might be necessary to kill Jimmy to keep him quiet. When asked who else knew about the discussions to kill Jimmy, Rummel replied, "Everybody involved with the case was aware of it." In his testimony, Stotler, while claiming that he and Jimmy were "fairly good friends," admitted he knew what Rummel was thinking. Even Burris, according to Rummel, knew that killing his childhood friend was under consideration. Advocating for the lesser of two evils, Burris told Rummel he believed Jimmy would be willing to accept a $10,000 bribe.

By early July 1980, Ischy visited Rummel at his residence daily to discuss the Jimmy problem. They knew Jimmy was due to appear before the federal grand jury in Austin on July 15. On Wednesday, July 9, Ischy told Rummel time had run out—something had to be done immediately. They decided to offer Jimmy $10,000, even though they did not have the money, and if that failed, more drastic measures would be taken.

Ischy believed that if it became necessary to kill Jimmy, they could take care of it themselves. According to Rummel, Ischy claimed he had shot someone before in a prior drug deal, but he needed Rummel to help him obtain a weapon and a vehicle. Knowing that the plan was to find Jimmy and either bribe or kill him, Burris and Stotler told Rummel and Ischy he was in the Valley. On Thursday, July 10, after Rummel's efforts to raise the money failed, Rummel and Ischy decided Jimmy needed to be eliminated.

According to Rummel, Burris, who with Jimmy had been caught red-handed, agreed. Rummel testified that Stotler also assented to the plan. The hunt was on.

On Thursday night, Rummel and Ischy left Austin for McAllen in Rummel's brown, two-toned pickup truck. They stopped in San Antonio long enough for Ischy to borrow money and a weapon, a .45-caliber pistol. On arriving in McAllen early Friday morning, Rummel and Ischy met up with Stotler and searched for Jimmy. They drove for several hours but had no luck. Tired and frustrated, Rummel and Ischy checked into a motel.

At nine o'clock in the morning on Friday, July 11, 1980, Rummel registered at a Holiday Inn under the name Bruce W. Reed and paid in cash. If needed, he could produce a false birth certificate, driver's license and social security card in that name. Ischy, too, used an alias. They did not want to leave a paper trail proving their presence in the Valley. Burris and Stotler continued the search for Jimmy while Rummel and Ischy slept.

The week before he was due to testify before the grand jury, Jimmy stayed with a friend in the rural area west of McAllen. Besides a trip to town to visit his mother, he spent most of the time at his friend's house. Although aware

Split Rail Bar, Edinburg, Texas. *Obtained via FOIA request from the United States Department of Justice.*

that his accomplices did not want to be implicated by his testimony, he had no reason to believe that they were considering killing him. On Friday, July 11, Jimmy drove to a country-western bar in Edinburg, the Split Rail—coincidentally, one of Kevin Frase's hangouts. Burris and Stotler found him there and told Ischy and Rummel. They met up at the Split Rail.

Stotler went inside to talk to Jimmy. According to Stotler, the conversation with Jimmy did not get far. When he approached Jimmy, he was confronted by a large man he assumed was a bodyguard. Jimmy intervened and told the man Stotler was a friend. Stotler indicated that he and Jimmy spoke only momentarily; then Stotler left. Both Jimmy and Stotler testified at Walker's trial, but predictably, neither man attested that a bribe had been discussed. For them to acknowledge that they talked about giving or taking a bribe to thwart a criminal investigation would make both men look bad in the eyes of the jury.

When Stotler exited the Split Rail without Jimmy's agreement not to testify, Ischy and Rummel knew what had to be done. At Walker's trial, Rummel testified:

> RUMMEL: *I was not successful in obtaining anywhere near* [the $10,000] *I would need. And it was decided that the only option left was to do it ourselves.*
> PIERCE: *To do what?*
> RUMMEL: *Kill him.*
> PIERCE: *And who was a party to that agreement?*
> RUMMEL: *At that particular time, it was Mr. Burris and Mr. Stotler and myself and Mr. Ischy.*

Stotler testified that in "no way, shape or form" did he plan or plot to kill Jimmy. He did admit that he attempted to locate Jimmy to facilitate payment of the bribe. He also acknowledged he knew that Rummel had talked about killing Jimmy, but he chose not to tell his "good friend" what Rummel was planning. According to Rummel, Stotler wanted to distance himself from any harm inflicted on Jimmy. Rummel stated:

> *When Stotler came out, he was already aware that something was going to happen. And he was very nervous and said that since he was identified by—or he* [had] *seen or talked to* [Jimmy] *and other people had seen him talk to* [Jimmy], *that he felt that he should leave and go somewhere and get an alibi.*

The amateur assassins waited for Jimmy to come out of the bar.

The Split Rail closed shortly after midnight. When Jimmy exited the bar, they followed him. Ischy, with the .45-caliber pistol, was in one vehicle. Rummel was in a different car with a 9-millimeter automatic pistol and his .30-30 rifle. During the pursuit, Ischy took a "pot shot" at Jimmy's vehicle from a distance. Rummel testified:

> PIERCE: *And how was that done?*
> RUMMEL: *From a long ways behind him from just out of the car.*
> PIERCE: *You were where?*
> RUMMEL: *I was behind Mr. Ischy.*
> PIERCE: *And what was the results of that?*
> RUMMEL: *Nothing.*
> PIERCE: *What happened to the car* [Jimmy] *was in?*
> RUMMEL: *I don't think he ever knew it. He (Ischy) was several hundred yards in front of me, and he told me he was trying to shoot the tire.*

Rummel and Ischy followed Jimmy to a rural residence. They discussed the possibility of going into the house but wisely rejected that notion. They waited several hours, hoping Jimmy would come outside or leave the residence. If he did, they planned to shoot him. After the lights in the house went out, they departed, believing Jimmy was in for the night.

Frustrated by their inability to eliminate Jimmy, Rummel and Ischy returned to the motel in the early morning of Saturday, July 12. Later that day, they returned to the house from the night before, but Jimmy was gone; they had lost him. Rummel and Ischy met with Stotler for lunch and discussed their next move. They checked out of the motel and set up a base at the apartment of Stotler's girlfriend. Search efforts by Stotler, Ischy and Burris proved fruitless.

The failures of Rummel, Burris, Stotler and Ischy made it abundantly clear to Rummel that they had no clue what they were doing. Rummel testified that Ischy's random shot at Jimmy's car

> *made me aware of the fact, I did not have any idea how to go about assassinating someone. And I did not feel that Mr. Ischy did either. What I mean, do it and get away with it. And I discussed this with Mr. Stotler, and Mr. Stotler agreed with me none of us really had what you would call sufficient knowledge to do something like this and get away with it.*

According to Rummel, they decided to contact a professional killer. Rummel started making calls.

Rummel believed Lloyd Chris Walker was the man they needed. Walker had previously bragged to Rummel that he had killed people during the Vietnam War and was "not opposed to doing so" again. Rummel stated that Walker also boasted about "influencing people to pay money" they owed and providing services for drug dealers "that would require something of a violent nature"—specifically (in the only instance about which Rummel could remember), shooting a person in both knees.

Rummel recalled a particular incident that occurred in the months before July 1980 involving Walker that lent credence to his claims. Stotler and Rummel needed to retrieve Stotler's pickup truck from an individual who had taken it without Stotler's permission. Rummel encountered Walker at an Austin bar and asked for Walker's assistance, fearing the individual who took the truck might be violent. Walker agreed to come along as armed protection. During that incident, Rummel told Walker that he was having trouble with someone—Jimmy—who might testify against several people. Walker replied that if Rummel needed his help, to let him know.

On Saturday, July 12, Rummel contacted Walker through another individual in Austin. They spoke briefly on the phone. During the call, Rummel did not expressly tell Walker he wanted to kill anyone. He explained that, according to the drug dealer "code of ethics," serious matters are not discussed over the telephone. Rummel only told Walker he needed his assistance immediately. Because of the prior conversation about the problem with Jimmy, Walker undoubtedly knew what he meant. Walker agreed to help, and Rummel arranged to bring him to the Valley.

Again using the alias Reed, Rummel chartered a flying service in Harlingen, Texas, to pick up Walker in Austin and fly him to McAllen. He told the service that his mother was ill and he needed to fly his brother down to the Valley immediately. Rummel called Walker and told him to meet the plane at the Ragsdale East FBO at the Robert Mueller Airport in Austin. The conspirators were so destitute that Walker paid the $360 charge for the flight. While Walker intended to be paid for his services, he and Rummel did not initially discuss the fee.

Even with a hired assassin, the plot to kill Jimmy was unprepared and haphazard. Though Walker wanted Rummel to believe he was a "professional hit man," he had no specific plan. They did not discuss how Walker would kill Jimmy; Rummel left that to Walker. On the phone, Walker, the hit man, asked Rummel if he should bring anything to the Valley, presumably referring to weapons. Rummel said no, they had what was needed: a .30-30 rifle and ammunition. Walker did bring several "special" handgun bullets of various calibers—.45, .357 and 9-millimeter—but no handgun that matched any of the bullets and no rifle ammunition.

The flight between the Valley and Austin took an hour and a half each way. Three individuals, including Walker, met the plane at the Austin airport. Consistent with Rummel's explanation to the flying service, Walker identified himself to the pilot by the name of Reed and said he was the passenger going to McAllen. The plane arrived in McAllen at about one thirty in the morning on Sunday, July 13, and was met by Rummel. While Rummel and Walker drove to the apartment of Stotler's girlfriend—no longer constrained by the lack of telephone privacy—they freely discussed what Rummel needed him to do.

Rummel testified:

> We just discussed the fact [a] number of people were going to be testified against by [Jimmy] and that at that point, I did not have the finances, or the people involved could not come up with the finances to buy the witness off, and that we were willing to pay to have the witness killed.

Regarding the time frame, Rummel told Walker that he needed to do the job quickly. Jimmy and Burris would be driving to Austin on Monday before their Tuesday grand jury appearance, so Walker needed to eliminate Jimmy within twenty-four hours.

Cautious, Walker wanted more information. Specifically, he asked Rummel who had something to lose if Jimmy testified and who would provide the money for his fee. Rummel named the other Loop 360 Deal conspirators. Walker knew Rummel and Stotler but not the others. Then, they discussed a price and agreed that Walker would be paid $10,000 once there was proof Jimmy was dead. Although they did not have the cash in hand, Rummel assured Walker the conspirators had the means to pay him.

Rummel, Ischy and Stotler would be responsible for paying Walker's fee. They expected no contribution from Burris, whose white pickup camper had been confiscated by police in October 1979 with the load of marijuana. Once Jimmy was killed, Rummel intended to sell his pickup truck to provide a significant part of Walker's fee. As with most of the murder scheme, both Rummel and Walker were unconcerned about the details. Presumably, Walker was not worried that Rummel and his friends would attempt to cheat an assassin out of his money.

La Quinta Motel, McAllen, Texas. *Obtained via FOIA request from the United States Department of Justice.*

Not entirely trusting that Walker would accomplish the mission, Rummel and Ischy formed a backup plan. According to Rummel, Ischy arranged for a second hit man out of Houston to kill Jimmy in Austin. The conspirators knew Jimmy would meet with his attorney on Monday before the Tuesday grand jury session. Should Jimmy still be alive at that point, the Houston hit man would kill him outside his lawyer's office.

Walker and Rummel drove to the house where Rummel and Ischy last saw Jimmy on Friday night. They waited for a while, but no one showed up. In the early morning hours of July 13, Walker and Rummel checked into Room 304 of a La Quinta Motel and went to sleep. Ischy and Stotler kept searching for Jimmy.

In the afternoon of July 13, Rummel met with Burris outside a McAllen Dairy Queen; Walker waited inside. Burris was upset. He blamed Rummel for letting the situation drag on and agreeing to pay Walker so much. According to Rummel, Burris claimed he knew a Mexican national who would kill Jimmy for less money. Despite his assurance to Rummel not to identify the Loop 360 Deal conspirators, Burris feared that his testimony to the grand jury would get him in trouble. If he and Jimmy testified to different facts, Burris could be charged with perjury. Rummel reassured Burris that he had the situation under control. Walker's name was not mentioned, but Rummel said someone was in town to do the job. Ischy and Stotler had been unable to locate Jimmy, but Burris believed he knew where to look.

Room 304, La Quinta Motel, McAllen, Texas. *Obtained via FOIA request from the United States Department of Justice.*

On Sunday, July 13, around three or four o'clock in the afternoon, Ischy took the 9-millimeter and drove back to Austin to make the arrangements with the backup assassin from Houston. Walker and Rummel returned to the motel and waited. Late in the afternoon, Rummel received a telephone call from Burris. He located Jimmy at Pepe's and believed he would be there for a while. Rummel and Walker drove the pickup truck to Pepe's; the .30-30 rifle was under the front seat. From the parking lot, Rummel could see Jimmy standing in front of the band among a group of people dancing and talking, and he pointed him out to Walker. Rummel would get no closer. He did not want Jimmy or anyone else to see him at Pepe's.

Believing that no one in Pepe's would notice him, Walker paid the cover charge and entered the bar, posing as an ordinary Sunday customer. He sat at a table near one of the mobile trailers, drank beer and socialized. Carelessly, he tossed his beer cans on the floor. Standing nearby, Jimmy had no idea that the man who intended to kill him that night was watching him and contemplating the best time and manner of accomplishing his mission.

Dairy Queen where Boyce Wayne Rummel and John Christopher Burris met while Lloyd Chris Walker waited inside. *Obtained via FOIA request from the United States Department of Justice.*

Charlotte and Kevin were socializing, too, totally unaware of the drama that would end their lives in a few short hours.

Walker returned to the truck. Close to midnight, after hours of futile waiting, he told Rummel to start the engine. Walker took the .30-30 from under the seat, leaned out the passenger window and fired. Immediately, he told Rummel to go. On the way out of the Pepe's parking lot, Rummel, whose view of the bar was obstructed, asked Walker what happened. Walker said he thought their problems were over, but he could not be sure. According to Rummel:

> He said something or mentioned something about seeing them fall or seeing him fall, I don't remember his exact words, and he said he had the guy in his sights after he looked into the scope again, and the guy was gone.

Rummel and Walker could not wait for confirmation that Jimmy had been killed; they needed to get out of town. They drove to the motel to retrieve Walker's belongings, then straight back to Austin. When he dropped Walker off at his house, Rummel told him that he would get his money as soon as there was proof that Jimmy was dead. Walker kept the murder weapon.

Back in Austin, Rummel had no idea if Jimmy was still alive. He called Stotler, who remained in the Valley, but he, too, was in the dark. There was nothing in the McAllen newspaper about the shooting. Before noon on Monday, July 14, Rummel learned something had "gone wrong." Two people had been killed, and Rummel could not be sure that one of them was Jimmy.

The next day, Tuesday, July 15, Ischy appeared at Rummel's house in Austin. He said a young man and a young woman, not Jimmy, had been killed at Pepe's. Ischy, believing police suspected him of being involved, went into hiding. Later that day, Rummel informed Walker that Jimmy was alive.

DEA special agent Braziel, the case agent on the Loop 360 Deal, was informed about the effort to kill the government's star witness. His drug investigations often necessitated waking Pierce in the middle of the night with requests to prepare search warrants. Braziel's call to Pierce in the early morning hours of July 14 was different. He told Pierce that an assassin had tried to kill Jimmy at Pepe's and killed eighteen-year-old Charlotte and twenty-eight-year-old Kevin instead. Jimmy was unharmed.

Braziel and Pierce discussed what to do next—about the Loop 360 Deal case, Jimmy and the murders. They formed a plan of action, and Braziel went to work. Protecting Jimmy was a top priority. Braziel and Pierce did not want him to be unguarded if a second attempt was made. Braziel contacted Hidalgo County deputies to safeguard Jimmy until Braziel could take him into protective custody. Braziel kept Jimmy at an undisclosed location to prevent another attempt on his life.

As Pierce lay back down to sleep, he felt a range of emotions—tremendous sadness at the deaths of two innocent young people and anger at the effort to undermine the Loop 360 Deal prosecution. Yet, there was also a tinge of excitement, as the stakes of the prosecution had now significantly increased.

Less than thirty days after the shooting of Charlotte and Kevin, Jimmy appeared before the federal grand jury in Austin and implicated Rummel, Ischy, Stotler, Servantez and Crisp as the remaining members of the Loop 360 Deal conspiracy. Pierce recognized the courage it took for Jimmy to testify. He could have chosen to remain silent and go back to jail under the contempt order rather than risk being killed. No one would have blamed him. Whether he testified because of the attempt on his life or despite it, Jimmy gave Pierce the information he needed to prosecute the other Loop 360 Deal participants. In October 1981, at Pierce's request, Jimmy's sentence was reduced from four to two years to account for his cooperation. Burris also testified before the grand jury. The hunters now became the hunted.

Chapter 4

THE BREAK

Jimmy's grand jury testimony focused on the drug smuggling activities of the Loop 360 Deal conspirators, not the murders of Charlotte and Kevin. Nevertheless, it is fair to assume that Pierce asked Jimmy to tell the grand jurors about the attempt on his life. Pierce wanted the grand jury to know that the men whom Jimmy incriminated in the Loop 360 Deal tried to kill him before he could testify. The effort to eliminate Jimmy as a witness was a probative indication that they were guilty of the marijuana conspiracy.

While Jimmy believed that the other Loop 360 Deal conspirators had targeted him, he had no specific information about the killer. At Walker's trial, he testified that, to his knowledge, no other members of the conspiracy were present at Pepe's that night. Jimmy talked to Stotler on Friday night, but he had not seen Rummel, Burris or Ischy in the Valley at all. Due to the nature of conspiracies and the criminal's desire for self-preservation, the conspirators would begin to turn on one another, and the killer's identity would be revealed.

Drug-smuggling conspiracies like the Loop 360 Deal are a gold mine of potential snitches. Usually, such ventures involve multiple people, including financiers, organizers, loaders, transporters and dealers. During his AUSA career, Pierce often sought the indictment of as many as twenty-five people at a time for one drug conspiracy. According to Pierce, the DEA would catch one of the conspiracy members and try to "flip" him.

While it is unlikely that a single individual, particularly one lower in the organization, can provide information about the entire conspiracy or identify all the participants, he certainly knows enough to chip away at the conspiratorial structure. Even a low-level participant can give agents leads about the location of stash houses, upcoming deliveries or other accomplices. Promises of dismissed or reduced charges or a lesser sentence are enticing, especially if the arrestee knows what prison is like and does not want to go back.

The first conspirators captured in the Loop 360 Deal were Jimmy and Burris, arrested in October 1979 for flying the marijuana into Austin. They were not "flipped" in the traditional sense, but their cooperation was obtained, nonetheless. Under the threat of continued imprisonment for contempt, Jimmy and Burris described the Loop 360 Deal to the federal grand jury and identified the other conspiracy members, including Rummel, Ischy, Stotler, Crisp and Servantez.

David Ischy would be the next domino to fall. Based on Jimmy's testimony and before a second indictment was returned, Pierce presented a criminal complaint to a United States magistrate, and a warrant was issued for Ischy's arrest. In August 1980, DEA special agent Braziel took Ischy into custody and brought him to the United States Marshals' Office at the federal courthouse in Austin for processing.

Typically, a defendant is booked into jail after processing to await his appearance in court. Few defendants have a lawyer at this point, and bond will not be set until they appear before a judge. The plea bargain process occurs much later, when the defendant is represented by an attorney and both sides have complete access to the facts. Ischy did not want to wait.

In the month between the deaths of Charlotte and Kevin and his arrest, Ischy had plenty of time to think about the failed drug deal and the events in the Valley. His and Rummel's efforts to prevent Jimmy from testifying had come to naught. Ischy knew that Jimmy and Burris implicated him in the Loop 360 Deal and that if he was convicted again, he was going back to prison for a long time. Not only would his parole be revoked, but his prior drug conviction also qualified him for an enhanced penalty on the Loop 360 Deal charges, making it less likely that he would be released on bail pending trial.

Also, Ischy was acutely aware that the attempt to prevent Jimmy from testifying led directly to the killing of Charlotte and Kevin. As did Pierce, he realized that the murders elevated the Loop 360 Deal to another level. Prosecutors treat drug smuggling seriously, but at the end of the day, they can leave those cases "at the office"—not murder. The need to solve murder cases and capture, prosecute and convict anyone responsible can consume agents and prosecutors. The egregious facts of this case—the killing of two innocent victims whose only fault was being in the line of fire—intensified the necessity and urgency of finding the killer. Ischy did not want Pierce or some county prosecutor holding him responsible for that crime.

Rather than wait in jail for events to unfold, Ischy told Braziel he wanted to make a deal—his testimony in exchange for dismissing the Loop 360 Deal drug charges. Jimmy and Burris had testified about the conspiracy's important details. Ischy knew he could provide little more helpful information in that regard. Although he could identify the financier, fear of retribution deterred him from that course of action. But Ischy did have valuable information he believed Pierce would want.

Through his conversations with Rummel, Ischy possessed personal knowledge about the hiring of the assassin. He did not know Walker's name, but he knew who hired him—Rummel. When Ischy was arrested in August 1980, no one had yet been charged with the murders of Charlotte and Kevin. The crimes were still fresh in the minds of police and prosecutors. Ischy needed to act quickly. The information about Rummel would only benefit Ischy if he, rather than Burris or Stotler, gave it to Pierce.

Although Rummel may have believed he and Ischy were friends, Ischy did not. The bond created by their time in prison and their joint criminal enterprises dissolved when it served Ischy's interests. If implicating Rummel in the murders made Ischy a snitch, he could live with that, so long as incriminating Rummel kept him, Ischy, out of jail. He believed that the information he possessed would be more valuable to prosecutors than getting another drug conviction. He was right.

While he was still in a holding cell in the marshals' office, Ischy told Braziel he had information he would only share with Pierce. Based on his prior experiences with the federal criminal justice system, Ischy knew that Braziel and the DEA had no authority to give him the deal he wanted. Ischy told Braziel he needed to talk directly to Pierce. Ischy and Pierce were familiar with each other from his prior drug cases and his reputation as an aircraft drug smuggler in the Austin area.

Braziel called Pierce, whose office was also in the Austin federal courthouse. Willing to hear what Ischy had to say, Pierce walked down to the marshals' holding cell. When he arrived, Ischy said, "I know who tried to kill Jimmy and who killed those two people, and I can get him for you." Pierce knew Rummel was part of the Loop 360 Deal, and he believed that the conspirators tried to kill Jimmy to keep him quiet. But he had no evidence linking any of them to the murders.

The investigation by the Hidalgo County sheriff into the murders of Charlotte and Kevin at Pepe's had produced no leads on the shooter. If Ischy's information was true, not only would it further that investigation, but it also indicated that Charlotte and Kevin had been killed by a hired assassin. Anyone responsible for shooting them had committed a capital offense under Texas law and could face the death penalty. If Ischy could provide information that led to the killer's identification, his knowledge would be extremely valuable.

Though pleasantly surprised that Ischy could jump-start the murder case, Pierce knew better than to blindly trust Ischy's word. Knowing that he can personally benefit by implicating others, a defendant may tell a prosecutor what he wants to hear at the expense of the truth. The uncorroborated testimony of an accomplice, particularly one who stands to gain so much from cooperating, must be weighed very carefully. Verification of the information is necessary.

Pierce considered information about the killer's identity so valuable that it warranted more than a lesser charge. He told Ischy he would "let him walk" on the marijuana case if he delivered on his promise. In other words, any charges against Ischy for his part in the Loop 360 Deal would be dismissed. Pierce certainly did not condone Ischy's marijuana smuggling, but if the evidence provided led to the arrest of Charlotte and Kevin's killer, it was worth the tradeoff.

Ischy was so anxious to get out of jail he was willing to waive his right to a lawyer and make the agreement directly with Pierce then and there. Although the two men agreed in principle, Pierce encouraged Ischy to talk to a lawyer before signing anything. Prosecutors must tread lightly when dealing directly with an unrepresented defendant. Defendants often claim misconduct by a prosecutor as a basis for overturning their conviction. Pierce did not want anyone to contend that Ischy's rights had been violated in obtaining the evidence about Rummel or the killer.

A lawyer was appointed for Ischy, and they conferred. Ischy, fearful that the lawyer might divulge facts to the wrong party and place Ischy's life in danger, gave him no details about the information he possessed. On August 15, 1980, Ischy and Pierce signed a non-prosecution agreement acknowledging that Ischy wished to proceed *pro se*—acting for himself—though he reserved the right to speak with his attorney again. In the world of criminal prosecution, Ischy was not naive. He knew his rights and would invoke them if doing so would better serve his interests.

In the agreement, Ischy agreed to debrief with the DEA concerning his illegal drug activities and his associates. Though he would escape prosecution for the Loop 360 Deal, Ischy bound himself to answer Braziel's questions about the drug scheme. His answers could bolster the testimony provided by Jimmy and Burris and aid in the prosecution of the other conspirators. Ischy would also be required to testify truthfully against his Loop 360 Deal accomplices.

In return, any charges against Ischy for his role in the Loop 360 Deal would be dismissed, and he would not be prosecuted for any drug-related activity arising from that offense. The agreement did not, however, immunize Ischy for any part he might have played in the shooting at Pepe's. Should evidence come to light that he conspired with Rummel to kill Jimmy, he could be indicted for capital murder. Ischy, no doubt, assured Pierce that he was not a party to the agreement to hire an assassin. He laid the blame entirely on Rummel.

Most importantly, Ischy agreed to cooperate with state and federal law enforcement authorities in their investigation into the assassination attempt against Jimmy and the murders of Charlotte and Kevin. Pointing the finger at Rummel would not be enough. Ischy needed to obtain more solid evidence. He agreed to act undercover to obtain statements from Rummel implicating him in the murders. Ischy even agreed to take a polygraph examination to prove he was telling the truth. If a capital murder case against Rummel or the killer went to trial, he would also be required to testify regarding what he knew about Rummel and the hired assassin.

The agreement between Pierce and Ischy had no bearing on Ischy's parole status. Drug smuggling was a clear violation of his conditions of parole. As a practical matter, Ischy knew his parole would not be revoked if the underlying criminal charge was dismissed. For the agreement to be binding on Pierce, the information Ischy provided must be sufficient to result in an indictment against the person or persons responsible for the assassination attempt. If Ischy failed to fulfill his part of the deal, Pierce could nullify the agreement and prosecute him in the Western District of Texas for his role in the Loop 360 Deal.

Ischy agreed not to disclose to anyone other than his attorney that he had signed the non-prosecution agreement with Pierce. Utmost secrecy was essential to prevent Rummel and the killer, as yet unidentified, from learning that Ischy was cooperating and that they had been incriminated. Pierce wanted to be sure that anyone responsible for the murders of Charlotte and Kevin was charged and arrested before having the chance to flee.

After the agreement was signed and safeguards were in place, Ischy told Pierce that Rummel hired the assassin. While Ischy could not provide the killer's name, Rummel's arrest would move law enforcement one step closer to knowing his identity. Ischy was released from federal custody. A meeting with Rummel was arranged, and Braziel fit Ischy with a hidden voice recorder.

On the pretext of obtaining marijuana for personal use, Ischy called Rummel, who invited him to his antiques and restoration shop in Buda, Texas. When they met, Braziel was not far away. Rummel suspected nothing. As far as Rummel was concerned, Ischy was as guilty of the murder conspiracy as he was. Before the murders, they freely discussed concerns about Jimmy and what should be done to prevent him from testifying. When Ischy showed up at his door, Rummel had no reason to think he was wired and acting for law enforcement.

As they talked, Rummel indicated that he might need help collecting money from the Valley hit man—the first indication that one or more of the Loop 360 Deal conspirators had orchestrated the murders. When Ischy questioned the wisdom of trying to collect money from a known murderer, Rummel flippantly responded, "Well, I don't know why. He can't shoot worth a shit." Ischy carefully directed the conversation to the specific events in the Valley and the assassination attempt—not wanting Rummel to suspect he was acting undercover. While Rummel did not identify Walker by name on the tape, he made enough admissions to convince Pierce that Rummel had arranged the attempted murder of Jimmy, which resulted in the deaths of Charlotte and Kevin.

At Walker's trial, Pierce asked Rummel about the undercover meeting with Ischy:

> PIERCE: *And what did he produce for the Government, Mr. Rummel?*
> RUMMEL: *He produced a tape recording with myself and him in a conversation concerning this killing in Hidalgo County.*
> PIERCE: *What type of statements had you made on that tape recording that were made and recorded on that tape recording?*
> RUMMEL: *Very condemning statements.*

At Walker's trial, Rummel and Ischy told irreconcilable stories about Ischy's involvement in the murder conspiracy. Rummel not only implicated Ischy in the murders of Charlotte and Kevin but also made it sound as if Ischy was the primary mover behind the assassination attempt or, at least, was as guilty as Rummel. His testimony suggested that Ischy and the financier were pushing hard for action to ensure Jimmy did not testify.

Walker's lawyer called Ischy as a witness to deny Rummel's allegations and show the jury Rummel was lying. Ischy used the opportunity to refute Rummel's claim that other members of the Loop 360 Deal conspiracy were part of the murder conspiracy. He testified that neither he, Burris nor Stotler played any part in the decision to kill Jimmy. Ischy acknowledged the effort to bribe Jimmy with $10,000 but nothing more. His testimony indicated that he wanted to stop Jimmy from testifying but had not agreed with Rummel to kill him.

If Ischy did not participate in the murder conspiracy, why would Rummel implicate him? He certainly had the motivation to do so. As far as Rummel was concerned, his "friend" had stabbed him in the back. Pierce would not have known who hired Walker without Ischy's willingness to secretly record their conversation. Perhaps Rummel lied about Ischy's involvement in the assassination attempt as payback for the undercover tape.

On the other hand, if Rummel was telling the truth and Ischy did agree to kill Jimmy, why would Ischy cooperate and lead Pierce to Rummel, the one person who, more than any other, could say that Ischy agreed to hire the hit man? Maybe Ischy feared either Stotler or Burris would finger Rummel and he, Ischy, would lose the chance to plea bargain for dismissal of his Loop 360 Deal charges. Perhaps Ischy was so desperate to stay out of jail that he was willing to risk being implicated by Rummel. Ischy knew there was no direct evidence linking him to Walker. It would be Rummel's word against Ischy's. In any event, nothing on the undercover tape was sufficient to convince Pierce that Ischy—or, for that matter, any other Loop 360 Deal conspirator—should also be prosecuted for the murders.

In November 1980, based on Jimmy's grand jury testimony, Rummel, Stotler, Servantez and Crisp were indicted for conspiracy to import four hundred pounds of marijuana and for the importation of four hundred pounds of marijuana. Although the evidence at Jimmy's trial had been insufficient to establish importation (and he could not be retried for that offense), his grand jury testimony provided direct evidence that he had flown the marijuana into the United States from Mexico as part of the conspiracy. In recognition of Ischy's cooperation and in compliance with the non-prosecution agreement, he was not included as a defendant in the second Loop 360 Deal indictment.

In addition to having an "open and shut" case on the Loop 360 Deal conspiracy, Pierce possessed evidence strongly implicating at least one person—Rummel—in the murders of Charlotte and Kevin. Whether the latter case would be pursued in federal court remained to be decided.

Usually, state courts handle violent crimes, but here, an attempt had been made to kill a federal witness. Although the federal government possessed a strong interest in prosecuting the person responsible, Pierce wanted more than a conviction for conspiracy to prevent a witness from testifying. He believed that the assassin and anyone else who participated in the decision that led to the murders of Charlotte and Kevin should get the death penalty.

Pierce knew that Rummel would not face capital punishment in federal court. In 1972, the United States Supreme Court held that the imposition and carrying out of the death penalty throughout the United States, in state and federal courts, constituted cruel and unusual punishment. Legislatures were, however, free to reenact capital murder statutes that complied with the Supreme Court's guidelines. In 1980, when the attempt was made on Jimmy's life, no federal statute carried the death penalty for the crime of killing or attempting to kill a federal witness. However, in 1974, the Texas legislature narrowed the scope of death-eligible crimes. As of July 14, 1980, when Charlotte and Kevin were shot and killed, a person could face the death penalty in Texas if he killed someone in exchange for the payment of money, precisely the situation that existed here. In the absence of a federal death penalty for the murders of Charlotte and Kevin, Pierce turned to the State of Texas.

Though Pierce was forced to resort to state courts for the capital murder charge, he had no intention of letting Rummel escape federal prosecution for the incident at Pepe's. In 1982, two years after the murders of Charlotte and Kevin, Congress enacted the Victim and Witness Protection Act (VWPA), which made it a crime to use physical force or the threat of physical force to influence or prevent the attendance or testimony of any person in an official proceeding, such as a grand jury or trial. But the VWPA was enacted after the fact and could not be used by Pierce to prosecute Rummel. He and John Murphy, who assisted Pierce with the Walker prosecution, knew that there must be a federal statute that would permit prosecution for witness intimidation but were not sure which one was most appropriate. They eventually settled on Title 18 United States Code Section 241, a criminal statute not regularly used by federal prosecutors.

Section 241 made it a federal crime to conspire to "injure, oppress, threaten, or intimidate any person…in the free exercise or enjoyment of any right or privilege secured to him by the Constitution or laws of the United States." The "person" being intimidated was Jimmy, and the right or privilege in question was his right to appear before the federal grand jury to testify about the Loop 360 Deal. The fact that he appeared under threat of contempt did not matter. Section 241 was enacted to punish "traditional" civil rights crimes—racially motivated acts of violence such as those committed by the Ku Klux Klan and similar organizations after the Civil War.[13] The statute rarely, if ever, had been used to prosecute persons who sought to intimidate a federal witness.

Because of the novel use proposed by Pierce and Murphy, they were required to seek authorization from the Department of Justice (DOJ) in Washington, D.C., to prosecute Rummel under Section 241. Some DOJ attorneys did not believe the statute was appropriate for an attempt to silence a federal witness. Pierce and Murphy persisted and convinced them otherwise. Though Section 241 did not carry the death penalty, imprisonment for life could be imposed if the violation resulted in death, which, in this case, it did.

By the end of 1980 and into early 1981, Pierce had a clearer picture of his cases. Jimmy and Burris had been convicted and sentenced for their roles in the Loop 360 Deal. The remaining conspirators, except for Ischy, were facing charges of conspiracy to import and importation of four hundred pounds of marijuana into the United States. The federal government would prosecute Rummel for the attempt on Jimmy's life through Section 241. At the same time, the State of Texas would charge him with capital murder in the deaths of Charlotte and Kevin. No one in the state or the federal government yet knew about Lloyd Chris Walker.

Chapter 5

FROM STATE TO FEDERAL COURT

RUMMEL

The Travis County district attorney did not need much convincing to prosecute Rummel for capital murder. The crime itself was particularly heinous. While murder, by definition, is always unjustifiable, the circumstances that "trigger" the crime can usually be understood. More often than not, the killer knows the victim, and some motive, such as anger, greed, jealousy or revenge, prompts them to commit the crime. Even the elimination of a witness before he can testify, while inexcusable, is understandable. But causing the deaths of two innocent people by violent conduct directed at another makes no sense.

On November 25, 1980, a Travis County grand jury returned two indictments against Rummel, one for conspiracy (the agreement) to commit capital murder and the other for the commission of capital murder. The United States attorney and the State of Texas, acting through the Travis County DA, made a public announcement about the break in the case. The conspiracy indictment alleged that Rummel plotted with "a white male, age late 20's, 5"10", 165 lbs., long blonde hair and mustache, whose name and identity is to the grand jurors unknown" to commit murder in exchange for the payment of $10,000. The second indictment alleged that Rummel and the "white male" committed capital murder.

The description of the killer in the indictments came from several possible sources. Tijerina described the "Austin-type" man as "a tall, slim fellow about twenty-five, twenty-seven [with a] long [blonde] ponytail, braided."

TIME 12:49 p.m./4:00 p.m.	MCALLEN POLICE DEPARTMENT	CASE # 80-26,484
SECTOR HOW REPORTED ☐RADIO ☐ON SIGHT ☐PERSON ☐TELEPHONE	INCIDENT REPORT	DATE OF REPORT 11/5/80

NATURE OF INCIDENT
Outside Agency Assist

OTHER REPORTS
☐ OFFENSE

LOCATION
Harlingen, Texas

☐ ACCIDENT

COMPLAINANT
Lt. J. Lara

☐ ADULT ARREST
☐ JUV ARREST

COMPLAINANT'S ADDRESS

☐

NARRATIVE

On above date, Reporting Officer was contacted by Investigator Rey Garcia,

Hidalgo County Sheriff's Office, and asked if I would accompany him to Harlingen to

make composite from a witness in a Sheriff's Office's case (Murder 7/13/80).

On 11/5/80, 12:49 p.m., Witness, Mr. Howard Taylor Dalmage Jr., ▮▮▮▮▮▮

▮▮▮▮▮▮▮▮▮▮▮▮▮▮▮▮▮▮▮▮▮▮▮▮▮▮▮▮▮▮▮▮ was

contacted and gave Reporting Officer a description of a White Male Adult whom he had

flown from Austin to McAllen on 7/13/80. This subject is believed to have been the hit

man in the murder. The following description was obtained and a composite likeness

was made of subject. Please see composite attached to this report. Composite formula

reading is as follows: BB04, HH146 one down, GG03, CC09, EE06, CC05, NN02.

Description: WMA, mid 20's, 5'9"/5'10", approximately 150 lbs., medium build, unknown

type hat on, blonde hair, round metal rimmed glasses (possibly prescription), mustache,

light beard, pointed nose, long face, pointed chin, was wearing a red shirt with an

off-gold colored vest (sleeveless), blue jeans.

RECORDING OFFICER	OTHER OFFICERS	VEHICLE IMPOUNDED ☐ YES ☐ NO

Above is a composit likeness of passenger in "Young Flying Service" flight from Austin to McAllen.

Above was provided by pilot of plane, Mr. Howard Dalmage, Jr. on 11/5/80 at approximately 1:00 P.M. at Harlingen, Texas.

Above composite likeness is of suspect in Murder which occurred on 7/13/80 at Pepe's by the River, Madero, Texas, Hidalgo County.

Hidalgo County Sherrif's Office file #

Composite put together by Inv. John Lara of the McAllen Police Department, Investigation Division.

Top: Composite description by Howard Dulmage. *Courtesy of the Hidalgo County Sheriff's Office.*

Bottom: Drawing of suspect. *Courtesy of the Hidalgo County Sheriff's Office.*

Howard Dulmage, the pilot who flew Walker to the Valley from Austin, also provided a description to police in early November, which formed the basis for a composite drawing. Finally, there was Ischy.

Around noon on Sunday, July 13, shortly before Ischy left the Valley, he and Rummel stopped to talk while driving in separate vehicles. Ischy knew that the man in Rummel's truck was the person hired to kill Jimmy. Walker stayed in the truck while Rummel and Ischy talked outside. But that was enough for Ischy to get a partial description. At Walker's trial, Pierce asked Ischy:

> PIERCE: *Who was with Mr. Rummel?*
> ISCHY: *I don't know.*
> PIERCE: *You had not seen him before?*
> ISCHY: *I just saw the back of their head.*
> PIERCE: *What did they look like? What did you see?*
> ISCHY: *A white male with blonde hair.*
> PIERCE: *What kind of blonde hair?*
> ISCHY: *Long.*
> PIERCE: *How was it fixed?*
> ISCHY: *It was stuffed in a baseball cap.*
> PIERCE: *Was it a ponytail?*
> ISCHY: *I think so. It was either gathered or stuffed back of the collar or something.*

The taped conversation with Ischy made it difficult, if not impossible, for Rummel to deny that he hired the assassin. So, Rummel's lawyer negotiated a plea agreement to save him from the death penalty. Just as Ischy's information about Rummel led to the dismissal of the Loop 360 Deal drug charges against him, Rummel possessed valuable knowledge the prosecutors were willing to bargain for—the killer's identity. Knowing Walker's propensity to resort to violence, providing his name to prosecutors was not Rummel's first choice. Nevertheless, partly out of remorse and partly to save himself, Rummel agreed to disclose Walker's identity.

In July 1981, one year after the murders of Charlotte and Kevin, Rummel entered into a plea agreement to resolve his capital murder charges, the Loop 360 Deal indictment and his yet-to-be-filed Section 241 charge in federal court. Pierce actively participated in the plea negotiations with Rummel and his attorney. The Travis County DA and the Hidalgo County DA were also parties to the agreement. Although no charges had yet been filed against

Rummel in Hidalgo County, Rummel and his attorney knew they could be. They wanted the plea agreement to include all existing and potential charges.

Most importantly, as far as Rummel was concerned, the capital murder charges would be dismissed in Travis County, and no similar charges would be filed in Hidalgo County. To ensure that Rummel was convicted in federal court for attempting to kill a federal witness, Pierce charged Rummel under Section 241. Under the plea agreement, Rummel would plead guilty to that charge and receive forty years in federal prison. Forty years was a long time but better than life. In the absence of a federal death penalty, Pierce was satisfied that the lengthy term was sufficient punishment for Rummel's crime. Rummel also agreed to plead guilty to one count of the Loop 360 Deal indictment, for which he would receive a five-year sentence. In recognition of Rummel's cooperation, Pierce agreed that the forty-year and five-year sentences could run concurrently; Rummel would be serving both federal convictions at the same time.

Pleading guilty was only the first step in Rummel's acceptance of responsibility. He was obligated to cooperate fully with law enforcement authorities in their investigation of his state and federal cases. As did Ischy, Rummel was required to debrief with DEA special agent Braziel concerning his illegal drug activities and those of his Loop 360 Deal associates. He would not be prosecuted for any other criminal acts disclosed by his cooperation. Also, he would not be forced to testify concerning illegal drug-trafficking activities involving his family. Just as relief from the death penalty was Rummel's most important consideration, the essence of the agreement for Pierce and the state prosecutors was his disclosure of the shooter's identity. That person, Rummel said, was Lloyd Chris Walker. Also critical was Rummel's promise to testify about his agreement with Walker and the events in the Valley.

The United States attorney, acting through Pierce, retained the sole discretion to determine whether Rummel cooperated fully and truthfully. If Pierce believed Rummel was lying or withholding valuable information, he could nullify the agreement. Also, should Rummel violate any of the provisions of the plea agreement, capital murder charges in Travis County could be reinstated or filed against him in Hidalgo County. If the deal fell through, his statements to law enforcement authorities while being debriefed could not be used against him at trial. However, his taped admissions to Ischy were still admissible and would be enough to prove his guilt and obtain a death sentence.

Soon after the plea agreement was signed, the Travis County capital murder charges were dismissed. While the plea agreement was quite specific regarding Rummel's obligations, criminal cases do not always run smoothly, even when the charges are resolved by agreement. Once Walker was identified, charged with capital murder in Travis County and arrested, Rummel was called to testify for the state in Walker's bond hearing in Austin in the summer of 1981. Rummel's testimony that Walker fired the fatal shot was needed to bolster the state's request that the amount of Walker's bond be sufficiently high that he would be unable to get out of jail.

Apparently, Rummel was not as forthcoming at the hearing as the prosecutor believed he should be. The Travis County DA took Rummel aside and reminded him, in no uncertain terms, of his obligations under the plea agreement. Before the events in the Valley, Rummel and Walker were "associates" when they accompanied Stotler to retrieve his truck. In July 1980, they conspired to kill Jimmy, stalked him at Pepe's, then fled Pepe's together after Charlotte and Kevin were killed. In the Austin courtroom, Rummel faced Walker as an adversary for the first time. He knew Walker was capable of murder. He had watched from the driver's seat of the pickup truck as Walker hung out the passenger window and fired the .30-30 into Pepe's, killing Charlotte and Kevin. Fear undoubtedly made Rummel, by his own admission, "hesitant" during his testimony. Eventually, he provided sufficient evidence to support a finding that Walker committed capital murder. Bail was denied.

The Hidalgo County DA learned of Rummel's hesitation during the bond hearing. He also discovered through an investigator that Walker's attorney visited Rummel in jail. Both matters gave the DA great concern. Trial lawyers strongly resist efforts by opposing counsel to gain unaccompanied access to their witnesses, especially one as crucial as Rummel. The DA feared that Rummel might decide it was not in his best interests to testify against Walker.

Despite the plea agreement that protected Rummel from prosecution in Hidalgo County, the Hidalgo County DA presented the case to a grand jury. In January 1982, Rummel was indicted in Hidalgo County for conspiracy to commit capital murder. So long as he fulfilled his obligations under the plea agreement, the case would not be prosecuted further. Until he did comply, the charge would hang over Rummel's head. The Hidalgo County DA did not want Rummel to have a change of heart should he be tempted not to testify fully and completely about Walker's role in killing Charlotte and Kevin. If Rummel faltered, the Hidalgo County DA would proceed against him on the capital murder indictment.

In August 1981, Rummel pleaded guilty in federal court before United States district judge H.F. Garcia to his role in the Loop 360 Deal and the Section 241 violation of attempting to prevent Jimmy from testifying.

Most federal plea agreements are not binding on a federal judge. Recommendations by the AUSA and defense attorney that a defendant be sentenced to probation or to a certain amount of time in prison can be rejected if the judge does not believe that justice will be served. As a former prosecutor and state district court judge, Judge Garcia understood Rummel's desire to know the sentence he would receive and Pierce's goal of identifying and prosecuting the killer. He accepted the recommendations.

In September 1981, Judge Garcia sentenced Rummel to five- and forty-year terms of imprisonment to run concurrently, as provided in the plea agreement. Although his federal charges had been resolved, Rummel knew he still faced state capital murder charges if he did not testify about Walker's role in killing Charlotte and Kevin. That possibility, no doubt, weighed heavily on him at the time of Walker's trial. Whether the threat of a capital murder prosecution impacted his credibility as a witness would be a critical issue for the Walker jury to decide.

WALKER

From the media coverage in November 1980, Walker learned that Rummel had been charged with capital murder in the deaths of Charlotte and Kevin. He was keenly aware that Rummel was the only person who could implicate him. But Walker also knew, based on reports in the newspaper, that authorities were looking for someone fitting his description. Less than two weeks after Rummel was indicted in Travis County, Walker left Austin for Ruidoso, New Mexico. At his trial, Walker testified that he did not flee to avoid prosecution but "relocated" because he had a job in New Mexico as a ski instructor. Despite his explanation, leaving the state so soon after Rummel's indictment appeared highly suspicious.

Soon after Rummel identified Walker as the assassin, a Travis County grand jury returned two indictments naming Lloyd Chris Walker as the man who fired the shot that killed Charlotte. Walker was charged in the first indictment with the commission of capital murder by shooting Charlotte in Hidalgo County while attempting to kill Jimmy for $10,000, to be paid by Rummel. The second indictment alleged that Walker engaged in a conspiracy to commit capital murder by agreeing with Rummel, while in Travis County, to kill Jimmy for $10,000. An arrest warrant was issued.

On July 20, 1981, Walker was arrested while working as a waiter at a ski resort on the Mescalero Indian Reservation in New Mexico. He told the arresting officers his name was Mike Walker, a name his family had called him since he was young. A search warrant was issued and executed for the trailer where Walker lived with his nineteen-year-old wife. In addition to a small amount of marijuana, officers discovered a .30-30 rifle. Rummel told Pierce that Walker used a .30-30 rifle at Pepe's and that Walker kept the gun after they parted ways in Austin. If the .30-30 rifle found in New Mexico was the murder weapon, the case against Walker would be open and shut. It was not the same weapon.

Walker's arrest outside the State of Texas added an extra step in his prosecution. He was entitled to an extradition hearing in a New Mexico district court. Walker, still in custody, appeared with an attorney for his extradition hearing but chose not to challenge his removal to Texas, for good reason. Prosecutors in New Mexico threatened to charge Walker's wife, who was seven months pregnant with their first child, with possession of the marijuana found in their trailer. In exchange for a promise not to prosecute her, Walker agreed to return to Texas.

Custody of Walker was turned over to Travis County law enforcement officers, who drove him back to Austin. Feigning ignorance, Walker asked about the charges in Texas. One of the Travis County deputies asked him if he knew Boyce Rummel. Walker said no, a denial that would backfire at trial.

Walker made his first appearance before a court in Travis County on July 24, 1981, the same date Rummel was initially charged in federal court. Based on Walker's assertion that he was destitute and unable to hire a lawyer, counsel was appointed to represent him. Although counsel appointed in capital murder cases are usually highly qualified, someone believed Walker needed to be represented by one of the most experienced and well-known criminal defense lawyers in the state, Percy Foreman, and was willing to pay the substantial fee. Foreman was a flamboyant and nationally renowned attorney whose clients included James Earl Ray, who pleaded guilty to the assassination of Martin Luther King Jr. in exchange for a life sentence. He also successfully defended Charles Harrelson on a murder charge several years before Harrelson killed United States district judge John H. Wood in San Antonio. Foreman briefly represented Jack Ruby following his conviction for the killing of Lee Harvey Oswald.[14]

One of the young lawyers in Foreman's Houston firm was Mike DeGeurin, a well-respected criminal defense attorney in his own right. Foreman told DeGeurin to go to the Travis County Jail in Austin and talk to Walker about representation. Though happy to have DeGeurin's representation in

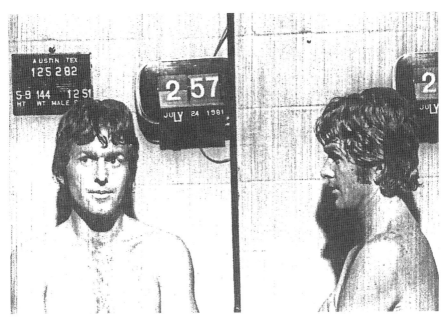

Above: Walker's booking photo. *Courtesy of the Austin Police Department.*

Left: Letter signed by Walker requesting Mike DeGeurin's representation and waiving any conflict of interest. *Courtesy of Archie Carl Pierce.*

1981, Walker would later claim that whoever hired DeGeurin had a vested interest in ensuring that he, Walker, kept his mouth shut and did not identify that individual to the prosecution—the inference being that Walker could implicate that person in a crime.

DeGeurin recalled his first impression of Walker as "handsome and well-spoken." On August 5, 1981, after conferring with DeGeurin, Walker signed a letter, dictated by Foreman, requesting that DeGeurin represent him on the pending capital murder indictments in Travis County and any charges that might be filed in Hidalgo County. The letter acknowledged that Walker had no money to pay DeGeurin, but that "friends and relatives" would help pay the fees. Walker expressly waived any actual or potential "conflict of interest" caused by this unusual third-party fee arrangement. While such legal jargon has little meaning to laypeople like Walker, Foreman completely understood the waiver's legal significance, which would become the subject of Walker's later attempt to overturn his conviction.

DeGeurin's first task was to get Walker out of jail. He did not want Walker to make some random, incriminating remark to a cellmate that could be used against him at trial. DeGeurin requested that reasonable bail be set. After conducting a hearing, which included testimony from Rummel, a Travis County judge determined that the proof provided by the Travis County DA established a likelihood that Walker committed capital murder. Bail was denied.

DeGeurin appealed to the Fourth Court of Appeals in Austin, which affirmed the denial on December 9, 1981. While seeking Walker's release from jail, DeGeurin also pressed for a speedy trial. Walker's case was set for trial twice, and twice the state filed motions for continuance. The DA was not ready for trial. Unable to obtain a bond, DeGeurin demanded that either Walker be tried immediately on the pending indictments or the charges be dismissed.

On December 10, 1981, the Travis County DA responded by filing a motion to dismiss the indictments against Walker. As the reason for dismissal, the motion indicated that, although Walker was in Travis County when Rummel solicited him to attempt the assassination of Jimmy, the location of the actual killing, Hidalgo County, was the more appropriate venue for prosecution. No mention was made of the state's inability to be prepared for trial. DeGeurin had beaten the Travis County case.

The Travis County DA and the Hidalgo County DA had been communicating. At almost the same time that the Travis County indictments were dismissed, two criminal complaints were filed against Walker in Hidalgo County, charging him with murder. Arrest warrants were issued, recommending that no bond be set. Walker was transported from Austin to McAllen to answer the new charges. On January 13, 1982, two capital murder indictments were returned by a Hidalgo County grand jury.

The first indictment alleged that on or about July 14, 1980, Walker

> *did then and there intentionally and knowingly cause the death of an individual, to-wit: CHARLOTTE KAY ELLIOTT by shooting her with a gun; and the said LLOYD CHRIS WALKER did then and there cause the death of CHARLOTTE KAY ELLIOTT by shooting her with a gun for remuneration and the promise of remuneration from BOYCE WAYNE RUMMEL, to-wit: $10,000 in current money of the United States of America if the said LLOYD CHRIS WALKER would kill (Jimmy) and the said LLOYD CHRIS WALKER in fulfilling his agreement to kill (Jimmy) did then and there fire a gun in the direction of (Jimmy) with the intent to kill (Jimmy) but the shooting of the gun as aforesaid did miss (Jimmy) and kill the said CHARLOTTE KAY ELLIOT.*

The second indictment alleged that Walker shot and killed Kevin in attempting to kill Jimmy for money. Again, no bond was set.

In Travis County, DeGeurin's insistence on a speedy trial for Walker had resulted in the state's dismissal of the indictments. Now, in Hidalgo County, he continued the pressure. In February 1982, DeGeurin complained about the state's failure to provide Walker a speedy trial. At the same time, DeGeurin asked the Hidalgo County District Court to release Walker on bond. In 1982, Texas law provided that, in a capital murder case, the defendant must be given bail if the state has been granted more than one continuance. On January 22, 1982, a hearing was held before the Hidalgo County district judge. The judge did not believe that the Travis County continuances should be counted in determining if Walker should be admitted to bail in Hidalgo County. He denied DeGeurin's request. DeGeurin appealed the denial, this time successfully. On February 18, 1982, the Thirteenth Court of Appeals directed that a reasonable bail for Walker be set.

Dissatisfied with the court of appeals ruling, the state initially appealed to the Texas Court of Criminal Appeals. The appeal would have delayed Walker's release for months, but the Hidalgo County DA inexplicably chose not to wait for a ruling. Instead, as had the Travis County DA, he decided to dismiss the capital murder indictments against Walker.

Pierce had relied on the Travis County DA to prosecute Walker for capital murder and learned in December 1981 that those cases had fallen through. When the Hidalgo County DA indicted Walker in January 1982, Pierce believed he would aggressively prosecute Walker for the murders of Charlotte and Kevin. Now, barely two months later, those cases were being dismissed. Not only did the Hidalgo County DA intend to dismiss the capital murder indictments against Walker, but he also failed to inform Pierce, who learned about the dismissal due only to incredibly serendipitous good fortune.

During the prosecution of Rummel for capital murder in Travis County, Pierce communicated with Joseph A. Turner, an assistant district attorney in the Travis County DA's Office, concerning the terms of Rummel's plea agreement. Turner also prosecuted Walker in Travis County. Following the dismissal of the Travis County capital murder cases against Walker, Turner left the DA's office and went to work for the United States attorney for the Western District of Texas, the same office where Pierce worked. He remained interested in the status of Walker's case and sought an update from the Hidalgo County DA. Turner called the Hidalgo County DA just after the decision was made to dismiss Walker's capital murder indictments and before the motions were filed. Turner immediately told Pierce.

On the surprise scale, Pierce registered somewhere between shocked and horrified. He needed to act quickly. Pierce believed Walker had fled to New Mexico when he learned about Rummel's capital murder indictments in Travis County. He was sure that if the capital murder charges in Hidalgo County were dismissed and Walker was released, he would flee again and never be found. The Hidalgo County DA was asked not to dismiss the Hidalgo County cases until a federal charge against Walker could be filed. He obliged.

Pierce presented Walker's case to a federal grand jury. On March 29, 1982, Walker was indicted in the Western District of Texas under Section 241 for conspiracy with Rummel to intimidate Jimmy in the free exercise of his right to testify before a federal grand jury. The indictment alleged that, as part of the conspiracy, Walker attempted to kill Jimmy, resulting in Charlotte and Kevin's deaths. Walker's federal bail was initially set at $500,000. A federal detainer kept Walker in jail. The Hidalgo County DA then filed a motion to dismiss his capital murder charges. Federal marshals took custody of Walker.

Whether by DeGeurin's design, the state's failures or a combination of both, the state capital murder indictments against Walker had been dismissed, and he no longer faced the death penalty. DeGeurin felt confident he could defeat the federal case, as well. Federal court would be different. DeGeurin faced procedural rules, a prosecutor and a judge, unlike in state court. Rather than a murder charge, Walker was indicted for intimidation of a federal witness. Pierce would not be required to prove that Walker intended to kill Charlotte and Kevin. However, he must show that Charlotte and Kevin were killed because Walker attempted to prevent Jimmy from testifying. As tenaciously as he had challenged the state indictments, DeGeurin attacked the federal charge.

Once again, DeGeurin's priority was getting Walker out of jail. Walker and his wife could not post the $500,000 bond. Even if the person(s) who hired Foreman and DeGeurin could help with Walker's release, the $500,000 cash bond was much too high. DeGeurin filed a motion to amend the conditions of release to lower the bond. He hoped to secure a personal recognizance bond or, perhaps, a bond that could be satisfied by depositing 10 percent cash instead of the full amount.

A hearing was held in early May 1982 before a United States magistrate in Austin. The sole consideration was Walker's risk of flight. To show that Walker would appear in court when required, DeGeurin pointed out that, despite a less than stellar record of behavior as a youth, Walker had no felony convictions. Walker's parents lived in Minnesota and would be unable to assist with their son's release. However, his stepgrandfather, David Taylor, could serve as a surety.

On May 10, 1982, the magistrate denied DeGeurin's request for a personal recognizance bond but lowered Walker's bond to $100,000, as DeGeurin requested. However, the judge did not believe that a 10 percent cash deposit of $10,000 was enough to ensure Walker's appearance in court. The magistrate noted that Walker was facing life imprisonment if convicted, which created a motivation for Walker to flee if released. The fact that Rummel had pleaded guilty to the Section 241 charge and would testify against Walker at trial gave weight to the government's case. Also, Tijerina's testimony and fingerprint evidence placed him at Pepe's, and Howard Dulmage would testify that he flew Walker to the Valley on July 13, 1980. The judge also noted that Walker had no ties to Austin, at least not anymore, and his work record was irregular. He had no one to vouch for him except his grandfather. More would be needed than $10,000 and Walker's promise to appear in court.

Neither Walker nor Taylor had the financial resources to deposit the entire $100,000 cash, and no one else posted the amount. Walker stayed in jail. The speedy trial problems encountered in the state prosecutions did not recur; it would not take long to get Walker to trial. His case, like Rummel's, was assigned to Judge Garcia.

Chapter 6

THE LAWYERS AND THE JUDGE

Pierce

Archie Carl Pierce, the lead prosecutor in the Loop 360 Deal and Walker cases, was born in Bryan, Texas, while his father was attending veterinary school at Texas A&M University. He grew up in the Galena Park/North Shore area of East Houston and attended the University of Texas in Austin, where he met his future wife, Jo. Displaying his typical wit, Pierce writes, "To the surprise of many, primarily my parents, I graduated from the university and was fortunate enough to be granted admission by the kind folks at the University of Houston to their very fine law school."[15]

Pierce had always wanted to be a lawyer and enjoyed law school. Applying himself to torts, contracts and criminal law paid off. He was invited to join the *Houston Law Review*, a distinction reserved for law students with the highest marks. Pierce was also admitted into the Order of Barons, the highest honorary legal scholastic society at the University of Houston Law School.

Jo grew up in the small town of Lockhart just south of Austin and did not want to live in the metropolis of Houston permanently. After Pierce graduated from law school in 1974, he and his wife moved back to Austin. He was hired as a briefing attorney for Judge H.P. Green of the Texas Court of Criminal Appeals, another distinction enjoyed by only the most successful law students. After his term ended, he secured a position as an assistant United States attorney (AUSA) for the Western District of Texas. Though Pierce would later attribute his advancement to good fortune, he clearly demonstrated a natural aptitude for the law.

Archie Carl Pierce. *Courtesy of Archie Carl Pierce.*

Pierce spent eight years in the United States Attorney's Office—seven years as a prosecutor in criminal cases. As a government prosecutor, he tried over forty jury trials and appeared over a dozen times to argue cases on appeal in the Fifth Circuit Court of Appeals. Besides the Walker case, one of Pierce's most notable trials was the prosecution of Jimmy Chagra on drug charges following the murder of United States district judge John H. Wood Jr., the first assassination of a federal judge in the twentieth century.

Chagra was an active trafficker of marijuana and cocaine beginning in the 1960s and, by the 1970s, was a well-known drug transporter operating out of Las Vegas and El Paso.[16] On May 29, 1979, Judge Wood, assigned to preside over Chagra's case, was gunned down outside his home in the upscale community of Alamo Heights in north San Antonio. Chagra was implicated. An assassination attempt was also made on the life of the AUSA assigned to prosecute Chagra. As a result, the AUSA went into hiding. When the United States attorney and chief of criminal section told Pierce he was now in charge of the Chagra drug prosecution, Pierce asked, "Is that because I am good or because I am expendable?" Just two years after joining the U.S. Attorney's Office and four years after graduating from law school, Pierce was handed the responsibility of prosecuting one of the most high-profile cases in the office.

Pierce was one of the most efficient and effective AUSAs encountered by this author in his forty-one-year legal career. Trained to think like lawyers, attorneys at trial often view their cases from the viewpoint of someone versed in the law, not as a juror sees it. They ask too many questions and make too many objections. Attorneys often find it difficult to combine their legal knowledge with common sense. As a result, the jury has difficulty understanding the case, which becomes more complicated and confusing than it needs to be.

When Pierce questioned witnesses, he would get right to the point. He did not ask unnecessary questions about matters that were uninteresting to the jury and immaterial to the case. In a drug case, Pierce would call the drug agent to the witness stand, ask the agent's name and occupation, then get right to the drug deal for which the defendant was on trial. The members of the jury only heard what they needed to know. Pierce's focus on facts essential to a conviction kept the jury attentive and minimized objections from defense counsel. Juries and judges appreciated his no-nonsense approach.

MURPHY

John E. Murphy, who assisted Pierce with the Walker prosecution, graduated from the St. Mary's University School of Law in 1972. Just out of law school, Murphy joined the Department of Justice (DOJ) Executive Office for United States Attorneys, which coordinates the activities of the U.S. attorneys' offices throughout the country. He spent most of his career in the United States Attorney's Office in the Western District of Texas as a trial prosecutor and supervisor.

Murphy started in the civil section with Pierce prosecuting cases filed on behalf of the United States, such as student loan, tax collection, antitrust and civil rights lawsuits, and defending claims against the government. In 1981, when the DOJ launched the national Organized Crime Drug Enforcement Task Force (OCDETF) program, Murphy was appointed chief of the OCDETF Task Force for the Western District of Texas. Eventually, he became the first assistant to the United States attorney, a position he held for many years through multiple presidential administrations.

By 1979, Murphy and Pierce were working together in the criminal division prosecuting drug cases in San Antonio. As Murphy said, "We grew up together, tried cases together, and made a lot of mistakes together." Battle-tested, they became good friends. Attorneys do not like to lose. Shortly after a defendant prosecuted by Murphy was acquitted, Pierce sought to console his friend by asking him to sit second chair in Walker's case. Murphy was thrilled with the idea and readily accepted the invitation.

Ordinarily, federal law enforcement agencies like the DEA and Customs Service perform the preliminary investigative work in criminal cases, questioning potential witnesses, taking photographs and securing physical evidence. Special Agent Dick Braziel of the DEA handled the Loop 360 Deal investigation, but no federal agency was responsible for investigating the attempt to kill Jimmy and the murders of Charlotte and Kevin. Initially, the Hidalgo County Sheriff's Office gathered the evidence and sought suspects.

While the Hidalgo County sheriff shared his investigative findings with Pierce and Murphy, they also made their own inquiries. They flew to the

Valley looking for evidence to help their case against Walker. They knocked on doors and drove around Mission and McAllen, searching for people who might know something about the murders. They went to Pepe's On the River to see where Charlotte and Kevin had been killed. The firsthand observations Pierce and Murphy made while visiting Pepe's proved invaluable. They saw with their own eyes the proximity of Pepe's to the Rio Grande, the open palapa, the levee and the parking lot from which Walker took the shot. Their knowledge made them better prepared for trial. They would need the advantage, considering their opponent.

DeGeurin

Mike DeGeurin seemed destined for a career as an attorney. His father was a lawyer, and DeGeurin spent time in his father's office as a child. His older brother Dick, who spells the last name DeGuerin, is also a criminal defense lawyer. The pair grew up in Austin, where their father was a confidant of Lyndon Baines Johnson. Dick specialized in criminal defense work, which prompted Mike to follow the same course. Mike received his college degree from the University of Texas at Austin and his law degree from Texas Tech University School of Law in Lubbock.

After graduating from law school in 1971, DeGeurin served as a briefing attorney to Judge Wendell Odom on the Texas Court of Criminal Appeals.

Mike DeGeurin (*left*) and Percy Foreman. *Courtesy of the Law Offices of Foreman, DeGeurin & DeGeurin.*

He served two years as a law clerk to United States district judge John V. Singleton Jr. of the Southern District of Texas before becoming an assistant federal public defender representing indigent defendants charged with federal crimes. In 1977, DeGeurin joined the law firm of renowned criminal defense attorney Percy Foreman in Houston.

Though overshadowed by his father and Dick, Mike DeGeurin possessed a little brother's determination. After Mike finished law school—far surpassing Dick in his grades—Dick offered to get Mike a job at the Harris County DA's office. Mike declined. He could not see himself as a prosecutor. "I can take the most awful person and, after thirty minutes with him, come up with more good in him than there is bad," he said. Instead, he went to work for Foreman as a defense attorney.[17]

In his own right, Mike DeGeurin would become one of the top trial attorneys in the United States. His work was instrumental in exonerating Clarence Brandley after ten years' wrongful imprisonment on Texas's death row.[18] Brandley, a Conroe janitor, had been convicted of the murder of a high school cheerleader. In 1987, Mike won a rehearing in Brandley's case. Ultimately, Brandley was freed due to DeGeurin's intense dedication to the case. His interrogation of the officers who arrested Brandley has been described as "breathtaking."[19]

Mike DeGeurin. *Courtesy of the Law Offices of Foreman, DeGeurin & DeGeurin.*

DeGeurin has "won numerous white-collar and corporate crime cases, including bank fraud, bribery, government contracting, wire fraud, money laundering and conspiracy. He has successfully represented many international clients in legal matters, including individuals and companies from Mexico, Canada, England, France and Germany."[20] His courtroom success has earned him many honors, including being named one of the *National Law Journal*'s "Top 50 Lawyers under 50," Outstanding Criminal Defense Lawyer of Texas by the State Bar of Texas and Attorney of the Year by the Harris County Criminal Lawyers Association.

One criminal defense lawyer described DeGeurin as "the criminal defense lawyer the rest of us want to be." A federal prosecutor he faced remarked, "I had the pleasure of trying two very lengthy and complicated federal trials against Mike when I was a federal prosecutor, and he was defense counsel. Mike has a keen intellect, bonds well with judges and juries, is highly professional, and is dedicated to his clients. He is one of the best and the brightest for high stakes litigation in this part of the country and a true gentleman."[21] Three smart and savvy young lawyers—Pierce, Murphy and DeGeurin—would walk into the courtroom for Walker's trial before a United States district judge unlike any other.

JUDGE GARCIA

To his many friends, who considered themselves fortunate to know him and be part of his life, United States district judge H.F. Garcia was affectionately known as Hippo. Though his given name was Hipolito, he grew into the moniker "Hippo" as an adult. Hippo was one of the most unique and interesting characters anyone could ever hope to meet in or out of the legal profession. His life was worthy of a book in and of itself. In fact, it became one. Based on interviews with relatives and friends, Joan Cook Carabin wrote *One-of-a-Kind Judge: The Honorable Hippo Garcia.*

Hippo's story is unique and compelling, beginning with his grandmother's emigration from Mexico and continuing through his appointment as the first Mexican American United States district judge for the Western District of Texas. After Hippo graduated from Brackenridge High School in San Antonio at seventeen in 1943, continuing his education was not his primary consideration. World War II was raging in Europe and the Pacific. Like most young men, he wanted to serve his country. On December 3, 1943, the day before his eighteenth birthday, Hippo enlisted in the U.S. Army.

After boot camp, Hippo joined the Third Armored Division fighting in France and Germany. He arrived at the port of La Havre, France, in January 1945 and, with no training, was assigned as an assistant driver in an M4 Sherman tank. When asked about his war experiences, he became quiet and reflected reluctantly, if at all, on the horrors he saw. He winced when he recalled seeing the bodies of young soldiers on the road crushed by tanks. The shock of war, the gruesome scenes and the frightening sounds of combat made a lifelong impression on the teenager. The emotional trauma sustained by exposure to death inevitably affects a person's future behavior, one way or the other. Hippo's compassion and understanding as a lawyer and judge can be attributed, at least partly, to his wartime experience.

Judge H.F. "Hippo" Garcia. *Courtesy of John W. Primomo.*

After Hippo was discharged from the army in May 1946, he entered St. Mary's University and, in 1951, received his law degree. He worked part time selling shoes and cleaning a car dealership to pay his tuition and bills. Though he passed the Texas Bar Examination, he did not immediately begin the practice of law. As a young man, Hippo was shy and lacked confidence. Law firms looking for assertive young lawyers did not hire him, so he worked as a deputy clerk in the Bexar County District Clerk's Office.

Eventually, at the insistence of his law school classmate Roy Barrera Sr., Hippo joined the Bexar County District Attorney's Office as a criminal prosecutor. Unlike many prosecutors holding positions of authority, he was neither aggressive nor overbearing. Despite legal training intended to mold future lawyers as hard-nosed advocates, Hippo's thoughts and actions were guided instead by his humble background. As an assistant district attorney, Hippo prosecuted individuals charged with various state law crimes but did his job with no malice in his heart.

Hippo's success earned him promotions from justice of the peace court to county court, where misdemeanors are tried, and eventually to district court prosecuting felony cases. Within eight years, Hippo became the first assistant district attorney and chief prosecutor. Hippo's simple manner of relating to jurors was disarming and alluring. Once, he prosecuted an individual for murder who was defended by his law school classmate and friend Barrera. Barrera was an eloquent speaker who used the better part of an hour to proclaim his client's innocence. When Hippo stood up to present the state's argument, he told the jurors he would take no more than fifteen minutes of their time because he would run out of English. The jurors laughed.[22]

To engender sympathy for his client, Barrera argued that his client was a simple man trying to protect himself from the overwhelming authority and might of the State of Texas. Hippo responded, "I am an overweight Mexican with a crazy-looking tie. Do I look like the power and might of Texas?" The jurors really laughed. He got the conviction.[23]

After serving twelve years as a prosecutor, Hippo briefly entered private practice. Within a year, Hippo placed his name on the ballot as a candidate for judge of Bexar County Court-at-Law No. 2. For the most part, Texas judges are elected. Though a lifelong Democrat, Hippo spoke to various community groups during his campaign, assuring them he stood with Democrats, Republicans and vegetarians.[24] He was easily elected.

Hippo was perfect for the bench. He demonstrated respect for everyone in his court—lawyers, defendants, victims and the families of both defendants and victims. His understanding and concern for the families of defendants, who in a sense were also victims of the crime, were passed down to others, including this author. Hippo was tough when he needed to be and compassionate when the facts called for leniency.

In 1974, Hippo was elected as a state criminal district court judge in the 144th Judicial District Court of Bexar County. The assassination of Judge Wood in 1979 created a vacancy for the federal bench in San Antonio. In 1980, United States Senator Lloyd Bentsen from Texas submitted Hippo's name as his replacement. Based on Senator Bentsen's recommendation, President Jimmy Carter nominated Hippo for confirmation by the United States Senate.

At that time, and still today, the appointment of a federal judge was a partisan process. As the 1980 presidential election neared, the anticipated election of Republican Ronald Reagan as president meant that Carter's judicial appointees would not be confirmed. As time wore on, Hippo's confirmation became increasingly in doubt.

President Carter's office suggested that Hippo contact his Republican friends and Texas Republican senator John Tower. It worked. Hippo's popularity crossed into both parties—all three parties, if you include vegetarians. His nomination was pulled from the pile of stalled Democrat nominees. In October 1980, less than a month before Reagan was elected, Hippo was confirmed as a United States district judge for the Western District of Texas.

Assigned to the San Antonio Division, Hippo held court as a federal judge two blocks from his childhood home on Lavaca Street. Hippo's criminal docket consisted mainly of drug crimes, immigration violations and weapons offenses with no identifiable victim. The absence of an injured party in federal court criminal cases made sentencing more challenging for him. Hippo said it was much easier to sentence defendants convicted of offenses when the victim had a name and a face.

Throughout his life, Hippo remained genuine and sincere. He exhibited compassion for those less fortunate—whether children in an orphanage or an individual from his own past down on his luck. Hippo was both religious and spiritual. Though he was a devout Catholic, his Christianity was not measured by the number of times he attended Mass or received Holy Communion. Hippo saw everyone as his equal, unselfishly gave to those in need and loved unconditionally.

Hippo mentored many Bexar County lawyers, many of whom became judges in either state or federal court, including this author. He was indescribably unique, with an unduplicated sense of humor. Many of his quips and stories continue to be repeated, bringing smiles to his friends twenty years after his death. Hippo engendered a reputation as a humble, dignified and fair judge throughout his legal career. In 2005, the federal building next to the Alamo in San Antonio was renamed the Hipolito F. Garcia Federal Building and U.S. Courthouse. Judge Garcia's patience, humility and common sense made him an ideal jurist to handle most cases, especially Walker's.

Chapter 7

THE TRIAL, PART ONE

The Prosecution and
Rummel's Cross-Examination

Although a federal grand jury in Austin returned Walker's indictment, his trial was held in the John H. Wood United States Courthouse in San Antonio. Due to the geographic size and the criminal caseload of the Western District of Texas, judges are often assigned cases from more than one division. Judge Garcia's chambers were located in San Antonio. In addition to his San Antonio cases, he was responsible for handling a percentage of the criminal docket in Austin. Traveling the short distance north was a welcome opportunity to visit with his longtime close friend James R. Nowlin, the U.S. district judge assigned to the Austin Division.

Walker's trial was scheduled to begin on June 8, 1982, a little more than two months after he was indicted. Despite the federal Speedy Trial Act mandate, criminal cases rarely go to trial so quickly. Trial continuances are requested for a number of reasons, including discovery, pretrial motions and absent witnesses. But DeGeurin did not need or want a continuance. During Walker's state court cases, DeGeurin had reviewed the evidence the prosecution intended to present. He knew who the government witnesses would be and what they would say. Pierce possessed little, if any, new information that would impact Walker's defense.

In the Travis and Hidalgo County prosecutions, DeGeurin's persistence in obtaining Walker's release from jail and his insistence on a speedy trial forced the state prosecutors, who were not prepared for trial, to dismiss the capital murder charges. Pierce, though, was ready. Judge Garcia resolved the pretrial motions, and jury selection began as scheduled. Fourteen jurors were chosen, twelve regular jurors and two alternates. Following jury selection, preliminary instructions by Judge Garcia and opening statements from Pierce and DeGeurin, the government began presenting its evidence.

Just as the memory of Charlotte and Kevin's deaths has remained with this author throughout his legal career, an extraordinarily thoughtful act by Judge Garcia early in Walker's trial made an indelible impression on the author and shaped his conduct as a judge. A child had been born to Walker and his wife in September 1981, two months after Walker's arrest. Walker's wife had no one with whom she could leave the child while attending her husband's trial in San Antonio.

Being nine months old, the child could not sit in court with its mother for long periods without requiring attention. A noisy child is a distraction and cannot remain long in the courtroom. Sometimes, the parent voluntarily leaves with the child, or as is often the case, a court security officer tasked with maintaining courtroom decorum insists that the child be taken outside.

So it was with Walker's child. Walker's wife, who wanted to be in court to support her husband, was required to regularly remove their child from the courtroom. As long as she remained outside, she could not hear the testimony, observe the proceedings and serve as moral support for Walker. Judge Garcia noticed Walker's wife repeatedly leave the trial. Sensitive to the feelings of the families of both victims and defendants, he knew being unable to sit in court was distressing to her.

The offices of Judge Garcia's briefing attorneys, including this author's, were equipped with speakers to allow his staff to listen to court proceedings while working on other matters. Judge Garcia offered his chambers, generally off-limits to the public, to Walker's wife. Immensely grateful, she accepted and sat in this author's office with her child during the trial. Because of Judge Garcia's extraordinary empathy and benevolence, Walker's wife could take care of her child while listening to the court proceedings.

THE PROSECUTION

In presenting the government's case, Pierce and Murphy each took responsibility for certain witnesses. As the lead attorney, Pierce handled the most crucial witnesses. Though it can be incredibly difficult for them, members of the victims' families are often asked to testify. The Frase family did not attend Walker's trial. Hearing about how Kevin was senselessly murdered at the hands of an assassin hired by drug traffickers was too much to bear. Both Joe and Gloria Elliott came from Rolla for the entire trial. They needed to confront the man accused of taking the life of their precious eighteen-year-old child. Pierce called Gloria Elliott to the witness stand.

A palpable feeling of sadness descended over the courtroom as Charlotte's mother rose and slowly walked from her seat in the back of the courtroom to the witness box between Judge Garcia and the jury. Only a parent who has lost a child could know how Joe and Gloria Elliott were feeling. The death of a child, especially one as young as Charlotte, is indescribably agonizing. Knowing the child was senselessly murdered is almost incomprehensible. No one in court could watch Gloria Elliott and listen to her testimony without feeling deeply sympathetic.

Gloria Elliott could provide no evidence about Walker's guilt or innocence, but her testimony impressed on everyone the catastrophic human toll taken by the assassin's mindless act. Pierce asked, "How many children do you and Mr. Elliott have?" Her matter-of-fact response hit every parent in the courtroom the hardest: "We have five children now. Six at the time of Charlotte's death." She identified a picture of Charlotte as she looked before the trip to McAllen.

Gloria Elliott explained that Charlotte had traveled to McAllen to visit her close friend Kathy Love. She testified that she and her husband gave Charlotte the trip as a high school graduation present. Everyone in court imagined the painful second-guessing that must have repeatedly entered their thoughts: "If only she had not gone."

When Pierce sat down, DeGeurin was given the opportunity for cross-examination. He wisely declined to ask Gloria Elliott any questions. She could say nothing to help Walker; DeGeurin might only make things worse. A victim's family usually believes the person on trial for the murder of their loved one is guilty. The wrong question from the lawyer defending the man accused of Charlotte's murder could prompt an emotional outburst that would engender the jury's sympathy and harm Walker's case.

Murphy next called Kathy Love as a witness to tell the jury about the night of July 13, 1980, at Pepe's. Kathy related that she and Charlotte had been together for several weeks before that Sunday and arrived at Pepe's in the late afternoon. As questioning turned to the events at midnight, she was forced to relive the overwhelming shock and sadness of seeing her friend, unconscious, lying on the floor. Murphy showed Kathy a gruesome photo of Charlotte taken after the murder. When Murphy asked, "Is that the girl you went to Pepe's On the River with?" Kathy could only nod. Kevin's friend, Daniel Harris, also identified a picture of Kevin taken after Kevin was shot.

DeGeurin strenuously objected when the photos were offered into evidence. Seeing a color photo of a body, often bloody, and its lethal injuries can have a significant emotional impact on unsuspecting jurors, who may become shocked, disgusted and angry. If the photos are admitted into evidence, the reality of the dreadful tragedy is imprinted in the jurors' minds. DeGeurin accurately described the images as graphic and "emotionally disturbing." But if a person can testify and describe a scene to the jury, then a photograph that reflects that testimony is admissible. Although the depiction of a murder victim from the death scene is usually graphic, a photograph supporting testimony regarding the injuries is admissible. DeGeurin's objections were overruled.

The government's primary witnesses were Jimmy, the intended victim, and Rummel. Pierce asked Jimmy about his involvement in the Loop 360 Deal, his subsequent conviction and the government's effort to compel him to identify the Loop 360 Deal conspirators. He testified explicitly about the events at Pepe's on the night of July 13 and how close he came to death. Jimmy also described his futile attempts to revive and comfort Charlotte and Kevin.

Rummel, not Jimmy, was the only witness who could implicate Walker, and Rummel's credibility would be crucial in the jury's deliberations. Pierce and Murphy presented evidence from multiple sources to corroborate his testimony. Telephone records substantiated Rummel's testimony that he placed several calls to Austin to obtain Walker's assistance in the Valley. One of the calls was made to a number registered to Walker's wife. The testimony of Howard Dulmage, the pilot who flew Walker to the Valley, established that Walker was his passenger on the Saturday night flight.

When Dulmage arrived in Austin, Walker introduced himself using the last name Reed, consistent with Rummel's testimony that Rummel, who rented the plane using the name Reed, needed the plane to pick up his brother. Dulmage testified he had no difficulty identifying Walker as the person he picked up in Austin. During the ninety-minute flight, which left Austin around eleven thirty at night, Walker smoked several cigarettes. Each time he struck a match, Dulmage's attention was drawn to the flash in the darkened cockpit, giving him a focused opportunity to see Walker's face. Dulmage picked Walker out of a lineup and then identified him again at trial.

Tomas Tijerina, the observant owner of Pepe's, specifically remembered an "Austin-type" man who seemed out of place and had described him to the Hidalgo County sheriff's deputies. When Walker walked into Pepe's on

Lineup presented to Howard Dulmage; Walker is second from the right. *Courtesy of the Austin Police Department.*

July 13 to get a good look at Jimmy, he had no idea he would be noticed among the many Pepe's patrons. But to Tijerina, Walker stuck out like a sore thumb.

In September 1981, over a year after the murders of Kevin and Charlotte, Tijerina was called to the McAllen Police Department to look at two groups of photographs—one set was black-and-white and another in color. From each set, he picked out the photo of the "Austin-type" man he saw at Pepe's on the night of July 13, 1980, and whom he described to Hidalgo County deputies. After Tijerina described this process to the jury at Walker's trial, Murphy asked him if he saw in the courtroom the Austin-type man he had identified in the photographs. Tijerina pointed to Lloyd Chris Walker.

Perhaps one of the most remarkable pieces of incriminating evidence was Walker's fingerprint on a beer can found at Pepe's. Tijerina had been able to describe Walker and tell the Hidalgo County sheriff's deputies where he had been sitting—at one of the two tables near a mobile trailer close to the parking lot. Amazingly, Tijerina also recalled that the Austin-type man was drinking a can of Budweiser.

The deputies photographed the tables, including Walker's, and gathered beer cans and bottles from the tables and the floor underneath them. The cans and bottles were provided to the fingerprint expert at the Hidalgo County Sheriff's Department. Some of the prints taken from the cans collected were only partial prints or were smeared and could not be linked to any individual. However, a readable, latent—i.e., not clearly visible—fingerprint was found on a beer can.

In 1980, unlike today, no national database of fingerprints could be utilized to match the fingerprint to a possible suspect; records had to be compared manually.[25] Jimmy told Hidalgo County sheriff's deputies that he knew the shot was intended for him and believed one or more of his Loop 360 Deal co-conspirators were behind it. Comparisons were made with the fingerprints of Rummel and Stotler, but they did not match. The deputies also checked the lifted fingerprints against those of local criminals, without success.

Walker was fingerprinted after his arrest on the Travis County capital murder indictment in July 1981. His ink-rolled fingerprints were placed on a card and later compared to the fingerprints taken from the can at Pepe's. The latent fingerprint taken from a Budweiser beer can on the table where Tijerina saw the "Austin-type" man sitting matched the right ring finger from the inked fingerprints of Lloyd Chris Walker. The fingerprint examiner noted fifteen points of comparison, far more than the seven points required for a match.

Attorneys will sometimes make comments or gestures not sanctioned by the court, to emphasize an important fact to the jury or even distract the jury when their opponent is trying to make a point. In Walker's case, DeGeurin cross-examined the fingerprint expert in an attempt to downplay the significance of the comparison, which showed a match with Walker's fingerprint. While DeGeurin was obtaining a concession from the expert that no fingerprints were taken from the tables or chairs, Pierce tapped on his water glass to remind the jury that the fingerprint was left on the Budweiser can. DeGeurin, who was focused on the witness, never noticed.

When Pierce called Rummel to the witness stand, he was escorted into the courtroom by deputy marshals. By Walker's trial, Rummel had been in custody for twenty months. In the fall of 1979, when he orchestrated the Loop 360 Deal, Rummel was confident and cocky, and in the summer of 1980, when he hired an assassin to take Jimmy's life, he was fearful and high on drugs. At Walker's trial, he showed no sign of his prior lawless arrogance.

Given time to reflect, Rummel knew that the murders of Charlotte and Kevin, unlike his prior drug crimes, were vile, loathsome and completely indefensible. He agreed to testify to save himself from the death penalty, but he was also ashamed. Accepting blame was one thing; declaring it in open court was another. As he sat in the witness box, it was difficult for Rummel, at first, to admit to a jury and a courtroom full of people, which included Joe and Gloria Elliott, that he hired the assassin who murdered two innocent young people. On the witness stand, Rummel spoke quietly—so softly that Pierce told him to speak up.

Experienced prosecutors have a good sense of which government witnesses are telling the truth and which are not. Pierce spent many hours talking with Rummel about the events in the Valley and believed he was "very, very credible." According to Pierce, Rummel was very forthcoming about his involvement and was remorseful for his actions.

Pierce believed that, despite arranging the assassination attempt that resulted in the murders of Charlotte and Kevin, Rummel was not a "murderer at heart" or "evil to the core." He was a drug dealer who had "lost his moral compass." Pierce knew Rummel was high on cocaine in the Valley in July 1980 and was extremely paranoid. But according to Pierce, his cooperation with the government and his admissions regarding the murders were sincere.

On the witness stand, Rummel started by reconstructing the Loop 360 Deal. He testified consistently with Jimmy but could provide more details, having been involved from the beginning and knowing all the participants. He explained that he and Ischy feared Jimmy would identify them. According to Rummel, their fear intensified as the date for Jimmy's grand jury appearance approached.

Next, Rummel related the events in the Valley on the weekend of July 11–13 and the unsuccessful effort to raise enough money to bribe Jimmy. DeGeurin objected to hearsay; he did not want the jury to hear about Rummel's conversations with Ischy, which indicated that someone other than Rummel planned to kill Jimmy. But statements made by conspirators during a conspiracy are admissible. DeGeurin's objection was overruled. Rummel then explained that once the conspirators realized they could not take care of the problem themselves, he remembered Walker.

Pierce asked Rummel why Walker was the person he contacted to eliminate Jimmy. Again, DeGeurin objected. He knew the answer and the damage it would do to Walker's case. Again, the objection was overruled. Walker had boasted to Rummel about killing people and providing "violent services" for drug dealers. Rummel also related Walker's assistance as armed protection during the retrieval of Stotler's truck. During that incident, Rummel put Walker on notice that he "was having a problem with a man that was going to testify against a group of people." So, when Rummel called Walker from the Valley not long after and said he needed his help, Walker knew why.

Rummel's Cross-Examination

One of Percy Foreman's maxims as a criminal defense attorney, which he undoubtedly taught DeGeurin, was: "You should never allow the defendant to be tried. Try someone else—the husband, the lover, the police, or, if the case has social implications, society generally. But never the defendant."[26] In this case, DeGeurin knew Rummel was that person.

First, Rummel was a convicted felon and admittedly culpable in the murders. Second, not only was he the government's key witness, but no one else—not Ischy, Stotler, Burris or even Jimmy—could say that Walker was the person who fired the fatal shot on the night of July 13, 1980. Third, Rummel implicated Walker only after making a plea agreement to save himself from the death penalty. His credibility would determine if Walker would be convicted.

DeGeurin subjected Rummel to extensive and pointed cross-examination to impeach his testimony in the eyes of the jury. He needed the jury to know Rummel had a reason to lie about Walker's role in the murder of Charlotte and Kevin. Rummel's motive was his plea agreement with Pierce and the state prosecutors. In exchange for his testimony, Rummel saved himself from the death penalty and limited the sentences imposed on him for the Loop 360 Deal and the killing of Charlotte and Kevin.

> DEGEURIN: *Now, wasn't the agreement, Mr. Rummel, that they would dismiss the charge against you wherein the state was seeking the death penalty?*
> RUMMEL: *Yes.*
> DEGEURIN: *In other words, to save your life?*
> RUMMEL: *That's correct....I made sure that it* [the plea agreement] *was inclusive of anybody* [including the counties of Travis and Hidalgo] *that could indict me on that case before I was willing to sign it.*

The plea agreement undoubtedly benefited Rummel, but it also hung like a sword of Damocles over his head. If he failed to comply with his part of the agreement, the Travis County DA could reinstitute capital murder charges, or the Hidalgo County DA could proceed against him under the indictment that was still pending.

The reason, contrary to the terms of the plea agreement, that Hidalgo County sought the indictment had a significant bearing on Rummel's credibility. DeGeurin suggested, correctly, that the indictment put pressure on Rummel to ensure his testimony satisfied the prosecutors in Walker's federal trial:

> DEGEURIN: *Do you have an understanding, Mr. Rummel, that if you please the government that they—that that charge in Hidalgo County will be dismissed?*
> RUMMEL: *I am under that impression, yes.*

The jury could easily infer that if Rummel did not provide convincing testimony that Walker was the shooter, Rummel could face the death penalty, giving him a reason to lie.

Under Rummel's plea agreement, it was not so much what Rummel said at trial that mattered as much as it was the prosecutors' perception of that testimony. DeGeurin did not let up. He asked Rummel who, specifically, would determine whether he had fulfilled his part of the agreement:

> DEGEURIN: *Is it understood that the United States Attorney has the sole discretion to determine whether* [your] *cooperation has been truthful and to the fullest extent possible. Now, do you remember that provision in the plea agreement?*
> RUMMEL: *Yes, sir; I remember that provision.*

Rummel acknowledged that, at the time of Walker's trial, he believed Pierce would determine if he had told the truth. Not only must Rummel testify against Walker, but the Hidalgo County capital murder indictment would also only be dismissed if Pierce was satisfied with that testimony.

DeGeurin's point had been made. Neither some objective legal standard nor a ruling by Judge Garcia would determine if Rummel had satisfied the terms of his plea agreement. Pierce would decide whether Rummel had fulfilled his end of the bargain. If he determined that Rummel had equivocated in his testimony against Walker or, in some manner, had jeopardized the government's ability to convict Walker, Pierce could invalidate Rummel's plea agreement, subjecting Rummel to prosecution for capital murder.

DeGeurin made sure the jury knew that Rummel must tell the truth as Pierce saw it, placing enormous pressure on Rummel—subjectively, at least—to say whatever was necessary to get Walker convicted. DeGeurin had no basis for believing and did not suggest that Pierce or the DAs in Travis County and Hidalgo County instructed Rummel how to testify. What was important was Rummel's belief that Pierce held his life in his hands.

In attacking a witness's credibility, a lawyer is interested in his state of mind during the events about which he is testifying. The passage of time can affect one's memory of the events, and the witness's mental or emotional state at the time can impair how he perceived the events. DeGeurin asked Rummel about his state of mind for another reason—to show he was so irrational and so desperate that he would kill Jimmy himself:

> DEGEURIN: *Were you under the influence of drugs while you were in the Valley?*
> RUMMEL: *During—*
> DEGEURIN: *During July of 1980?*
> RUMMEL: *Yes, sir, I was.*
> DEGEURIN: *In fact, you were heavily under the influence of drugs, weren't you?*
> RUMMEL: *Yes, in my opinion, I was as heavy as I have ever been.*

Rummel admitted he started using cocaine in 1979 and used the drug more extensively into 1980.

Rummel also acknowledged that he was under a great deal of stress at the time of the events in the Valley. DeGeurin elicited testimony that, at the time, Rummel was going through a divorce, and his antiques and restoration business was floundering. In establishing that Rummel's mental state was seriously disturbed, DeGeurin found support in the testimony of two of Rummel's co-conspirators. DeGeurin asked David Ischy:

> DEGEURIN: *What was the state of mind of Mr. Boyce Rummel back in July of 1980, in your opinion?*
> ISCHY: *He was out of it. I mean, he had been doing a lot of cocaine, and was just berserk.*
> DEGEURIN: *Was he rational?*
> ISCHY: *I would not say so.*

Sonny Stotler, who had driven the airplane seats from McAllen to Austin during the Loop 360 Deal and who, according to Rummel, actively sought out Jimmy during the weekend in the Valley, also testified about Rummel's mental state:

> STOTLER: *I have known Boyce Wayne Rummel for a number of years. He has always been a conscientious person. An unselfish person. I'd even say he was a benevolent-type person. The Boyce Wayne Rummel that I saw in the Valley and had seen prior to this particular date for over a period of months is not the same man that I had known for years. He was absolutely a different person. At times he could control himself, and at times he was out of control of himself. Like I say, a different person than I have ever known.*
>
> *I could tell he was going deeper and deeper—he was going into these depressive states or being pressured, you know, something along that line to say that he got to that fine line point to be able to assassinate a person, I don't believe that. I was afraid of him. I was afraid of David Ischy. I did not want to be around either one. I was in jail for almost two years, and I have seen killers, and I have seen the look in their eyes—I was very frightened for my own safety.*

Again, DeGeurin had established a valid and vital point for the jury to consider in weighing Rummel's credibility. Not only did his plea agreement give him the motive to lie, but he was also crazy enough at the time they were in the Valley to elevate his criminal behavior from drug dealing to murder. Rummel admitted his part in the decision to have Jimmy killed. Based on the evidence that he was desperate and out of control, little would be needed to push him over the edge to try to kill Jimmy himself. Rummel's paranoid thinking during the time made him dangerous. But suggesting that Rummel pulled the trigger is one thing; proving it is another. The only person who could say that Rummel went that far was Walker.

Much of DeGeurin's cross-examination of Rummel centered on David Ischy, whom Rummel testified played as large a part as he himself did in the decision to eliminate Jimmy. If DeGeurin could show that Rummel's testimony about Ischy was false, his implication of Walker would be weaker. DeGeurin emphasized during his cross-examination of Rummel that, despite Rummel's statements implicating David Ischy in the plot to kill Jimmy, Ischy was never prosecuted in either state or federal court for the crime. Along the same lines, DeGeurin asked Rummel about the status of Ischy's parole. Even if Ischy had not been charged with murder, parole authorities could certainly have acted on Rummel's information that Ischy tried to have someone killed. For a person's parole to be revoked, it is unnecessary to prove the violation beyond a reasonable doubt; a simple preponderance of the evidence is enough. Also, parole authorities can act without a jury. If the government believed Rummel was telling the truth about Ischy's involvement in the murder plot, revoking his parole would be the least the government would do. His parole had not been revoked.

Above all, DeGeurin made sure the jury was aware that no one else could testify that Walker was the killer:

> DEGEURIN: *Did you ever talk to Mr. Lloyd Chris Walker in the presence of anybody else that you wanted him to shoot somebody?*
> RUMMEL: *Not that I recall.*
> DEGEURIN: *Even though Mr. Ischy, Mr. Burris and Mr. Stotler and Mr. Crisp and Mr. X, do you know him?*
> RUMMEL: *Yes, I know him.*
> DEGEURIN: *And even though all of those people [were] down in the Valley at the same time, you never—no one was present when you had any conversation with Mr. Walker concerning shooting anybody?*
> RUMMEL: *That's correct....*
> DEGEURIN: *Is there anybody, Mr. Rummel, other than yourself that is in a position to say that Mr. Walker fired a shot at [Jimmy]?*
> RUMMEL: *Not to my knowledge.*

Aside from ensuring that the jury knew Rummel was the only person who could implicate Walker as the shooter, DeGeurin questioned Rummel little about the actual solicitation of Walker and the killing of Charlotte and Kevin. Perhaps a more thorough interrogation would have revealed a flaw in Rummel's story, but cross-examination on the details of the killing could also reemphasize those facts and bolster Rummel's testimony. DeGeurin thoroughly examined every possible issue on which Rummel could be impeached. If Walker were to be convicted, a failure to contest Rummel's credibility would not be the cause.

After Pierce and Murphy called twenty-three witnesses, plus two in rebuttal, the government rested. DeGeurin made a brief, half-hearted oral motion for acquittal, which Judge Garcia overruled. DeGeurin did not begin his defense immediately; he needed more time. Every day of the trial, Walker was transported from Bastrop Federal Correctional Institution (FCI), where he was housed, to the courthouse in San Antonio and back again, two hours each way. DeGeurin complained that he did not have enough time to consult with his client.

Because of the transportation logistics, Judge Garcia delayed the start of the trial to ten o'clock each morning to give DeGeurin and the marshals more time. Now, with DeGeurin about to present his case, he delayed the trial until the afternoon of the next day. He even called the warden at FCI Bastrop and requested that DeGeurin be allowed to stay later than regular visiting hours to confer with Walker.

Chapter 8

THE TRIAL, PART TWO

The Defense, Final Argument and Verdict

THE DEFENSE

DeGeurin relied on three witnesses for Walker's defense. He called David Taylor, Walker's stepgrandfather, to refute the suggestion that Walker was hiding in New Mexico using "Mike" as an alias. Taylor explained that since Walker was a child, he had called him Mike. He also testified that Walker left Austin in December 1980 because of a job in New Mexico. Next, DeGeurin called Ischy as a witness to contradict Rummel's version of events. Ischy tried to distance himself as much as possible from the violence. He testified that he did not know Walker and denied hiring him or anyone else to kill Jimmy. He also added that neither Burris nor Stotler had solicited a hit man. Ischy denied firing a pistol at Jimmy on Friday, July 11, as they left the Split Rail in Edinburgh and denied arranging for a backup assassin from Houston. He claimed that the possibility of killing Jimmy was not discussed until he and Rummel were in the Valley the weekend of the killings. If the jury believed Ischy, then the assassination was entirely Rummel's doing, consistent with Walker's defense.

On cross-examination, Pierce laid into Ischy. By agreeing to wear a wire during his conversation with Rummel, Ischy had played a vital role in the subsequent identification of Walker. But now, Ischy's testimony made Rummel look like a liar. Pierce wanted the jury to know that Ischy was the one who was lying to save himself.

Pierce asked Ischy about his prior criminal history—"three or four" prior felony convictions, all drug-related, all involving marijuana. Ischy also admitted that his failure to abide by probation conditions resulted in revocation. He conceded that by going to McAllen with Rummel, he violated the terms of his parole, which required Ischy to remain within the Western District of Texas.

Aside from his effort to evade personal blame, much of what Ischy said bolstered Rummel's testimony. He admitted being part of the Loop 360 Deal and confirmed that he met Jimmy when the plane with the marijuana landed in Austin. Ischy also confirmed that he was in the Valley with Rummel between July 11 and 13, 1980, two days before Jimmy was scheduled to appear before the grand jury. And he admitted he was present when Rummel discussed the possibility of killing Jimmy.

Ischy also testified, consistently with Rummel, that while in McAllen, Rummel used the name Bruce Reed. The managers of McAllen motels verified that an individual named Bruce Reed checked in at different times the weekend of the murders. Evidence showed that a person using the name Bill Reed also chartered the airplane in Harlingen, Texas, to fly to Austin to pick up Walker. Ischy acknowledged he, too, used an alias in the Valley to avoid identification.

Ischy admitted several other important facts. He conceded that he and Rummel were in the Valley to "talk to [Jimmy] and to possibly pay him $10,000" not to testify before the grand jury. Ischy acknowledged that Jimmy knew Ischy was involved and would implicate him. Pierce also established that Rummel and Ischy were the primary actors behind events in the Valley the weekend before Jimmy's grand jury appearance:

> PIERCE: *Tell us why you went to the Valley—tell us why you came with Mr. Rummel?*
> ISCHY: *Well, we had been talking about the case and what was going to happen, and we just got together and met and decided to go down there— he said that he could get the $10,000 and pay him off.*
> PIERCE: *Whose idea was it to go to the Rio Grande Valley?*
> ISCHY: *Both of ours....*
> PIERCE: *Well did you ask to go or did Rummel ask you to accompany him?*
> ISCHY: *I think it was just understood that we were both in this.*

Pierce then turned his attention to the talk in the Valley about killing Jimmy:

> PIERCE: *All right. And had you had any discussions at that point about killing [Jimmy]?*
> ISCHY: *Not as soon as we got there.*

Pierce: Had there been prior discussions at all about that?
Ischy: No.
Pierce: None whatsoever?
Ischy: A comment might have been made, you know, we could kill him.

Ischy testified that, on Saturday, July 12, Stotler, after meeting with Jimmy at the Split Rail, told him and Rummel, "There is no $10,000 buy-off, and he is going to the Grand Jury, and that is it."

Pierce: All right. So, what happened then?
Ischy: Just stayed there—that is when Boyce made the comment, "Well, for $10,000 anyway, I can have him killed."…
Pierce: Now, how was [Jimmy] *going to be killed?*
Ischy: How?
Pierce: Yes. There were discussions about that, is that correct?
Ischy: I understand that he was going to have somebody shoot him.
Pierce: How many discussions did you have down in the Valley involving the possibility of doing violence to [Jimmy]?
Ischy: Well, it was brought up, you know, a couple of times.

Significantly, consistent with the prosecution's version of events, Ischy confirmed that Rummel intended to hire someone to shoot Jimmy. He provided no support for the defense theory of the case and Walker's later testimony that Rummel shot Jimmy himself. Ischy's testimony, while exonerating himself from wrongdoing, proved that he and Rummel traveled to McAllen to pay Jimmy not to testify and that, once this option fell through, the decision was made to hire someone to kill him.

Then, when the opportunity presented itself, Pierce asked Ischy about the killer. Ischy testified to seeing Rummel with the hit man, and Ischy's description was remarkably consistent with the depictions of Walker given by Tomas Tijerina, the owner of Pepe's, and Howard Dulmage, the pilot who flew Walker from Austin to the Valley. Ischy did not help Walker's case as much as DeGeurin hoped he would.

After Ischy, Walker took the stand in his defense. He had little choice. Tijerina and Dulmage placed him in the Valley and at Pepe's on July 13, 1980. Walker needed to give an explanation for his presence other than the one proposed by Rummel. Both DeGeurin and Walker believed he would make a more credible witness than Rummel. He was intelligent and calm under pressure.

In the courtroom, Walker looked very respectable. Unlike the Austin-type hippie described by Dulmage and Tijerina, he appeared before the jury with short hair and dressed in a coat and tie. Though he was watched closely by deputy marshals, Walker, like most defendants in custody during trial, was neither handcuffed nor shackled, because restraints can reflect negatively on a defendant in the jurors' eyes and impair their ability to presume innocence. As the last witness in the case, Walker heard the testimony of every other witness before he took the stand. If necessary, he could synchronize his testimony with other evidence to ensure consistency.

Walker testified that he was thirty-one years old and was married with one child. He described his educational and employment background, which included training horses in Juarez, Mexico, across from El Paso, and his Vietnam service. Walker then testified about the events in the Valley, and he told a compelling story. He expressly denied being hired as the "hit man" to kill Jimmy. Walker attested that he did not participate in any effort by Rummel to prevent Jimmy from testifying before the grand jury. He also denied Rummel's allegations that he bragged about killing people and was willing to do so again.

As the fingerprint evidence and eyewitness testimony compelled him to do, Walker admitted he was present in the Valley and at Pepe's on July 13, 1980. Not only did Walker deny that he did the shooting, but he also gave the jurors someone else they could blame. Walker testified that Rummel, not he, pulled the trigger. Walker explained that he had flown from Austin to the Valley at Rummel's request to purchase a large quantity of marijuana. DeGeurin asked:

> DEGEURIN: *Did Boyce offer you anything you thought might be able to make some money?*
>
> WALKER: *Yes. He did.*
>
> DEGEURIN: *And what was the offer he was making?*
>
> WALKER: *Well, around Austin, from my understanding of Boyce, he was called a big-time dope dealer. He flashes a lot of money, and he claims he is from a family organization and by that, I don't know if he means a group of smugglers or it was his personal family, but a family organization that imports a lot of marijuana to the United States. And he told me that he was aware that I knew some wealthy people. And he thought we could make some money together.…He had been telling me at least two weeks and possibly three or more that he was going to be getting a large shipment of marijuana at any time, and that I should be*

available to come and look at it. And that would be essential. I would
have to see it and agree to accept it—the quality of it and the way it was
prior to him bringing it to Austin, Texas.

According to Walker, when Rummel called him from the Valley, they spoke about the marijuana deal, not Rummel's problem with Jimmy. He admitted paying for the flight and testified that he gave Rummel $3,000 to purchase the marijuana load. Walker also said they drove from the airport to an apartment complex to exchange vehicles and then to the motel.

At this early point in his testimony, Walker's version showed signs of cracking. According to the pilot Howard Dulmage, they landed in the Valley between 1:00 and 1:30 a.m. on Sunday, July 13. Motel records showed that Walker and Rummel did not check into a motel until 4:50 a.m. Walker's testimony did not account for this three-and-a-half- to four-hour gap. Instead, the later check-in time was consistent with Rummel's testimony that he and Walker drove around McAllen for several hours looking for Jimmy before going to the motel.

According to Walker, he and Rummel drove to Pepe's on the evening of July 13 to facilitate the marijuana deal. He stated that, after he and Rummel arrived at Pepe's, both went inside and sat down at a table. Walker's testimony provided an innocent explanation for his presence at the murder scene and his fingerprint on a beer can. But it created another problem.

Jimmy and Rummel knew each other from the marijuana-loading operation in October 1979 in Mexico. Rummel testified he remained in the parking lot because he did not want Jimmy or anyone else who might recognize him to see him at Pepe's. If, as Walker said, Rummel went inside Pepe's with him, it was very likely Jimmy would have seen him. Jimmy testified that he did not see Rummel at Pepe's that day.

Walker said that, after buying drinks, he returned to the table, and Rummel was sitting with another man. Walker, who had heard the description of the "Austin-type" man given by Tijerina, cleverly testified that the person sitting with Rummel generally fit that description. He wanted the jury to believe that Tijerina was mistaken when he identified Walker as the man sitting at the table; he tried to convince them the actual "Austin-type" man was the other individual with Rummel.

For his version of events, Walker even adopted the testimony that Rummel and the Loop 360 Deal conspirators tried to bribe Jimmy not to testify. Walker testified:

> *DEGEURIN: Did you ever see Jimmy at the bar or at Pepe's On the River?*
> *WALKER: I saw—well, I say it like this. I have never been able to identify Jimmy. When he walked into the courtroom here the other day was the first time I had ever seen him in person. But Boyce was highly upset when we got there, and he said, "There is that son of a bitch—that snitch."*
> *DEGEURIN: Did he point him out to you?*
> *WALKER: Yes, he pointed him out to me.…He did ask for me to speak to Jimmy for him but not participate in any type of violence. He asked me if I would offer the man money.*
> *DEGEURIN: How much money did he want you to offer him?*
> *WALKER: Ten thousand dollars.*

According to Walker, he declined Rummel's request; he did not want to get involved.

Then, Walker testified that Rummel left him at Pepe's for several hours. He said that when Rummel returned around midnight, he parked the truck close to the bar. Walker walked to the truck, believing Rummel had come back with a sample of the marijuana for the drug deal. Rummel had no marijuana with him. Then, Walker walked to the back of the truck to urinate. DeGeurin asked:

> *DEGEURIN: Did anything unusual happen while you were urinating in back of the truck?*
> *WALKER: As soon as I walked back there, there was a very loud explosion.*
> *DEGEURIN: What did you see happen?*
> *WALKER: I looked up and I saw a gun barrel going back into the truck. I was pretty shocked.*
> *DEGEURIN: Did you—did you—what was your immediate reaction at that time?*
> *WALKER: I ran back to the pick-up truck and said, "What the hell is going on?"*
> *DEGEURIN: What happened?*
> *WALKER: He said, "Let's go."*

According to Walker, he jumped into the truck, and they drove off.

Walker testified he looked out the back window but could not see anyone standing at the bar. He "hope[d] at the time that he [Rummel] had not hit anyone—had not shot anyone." When they reached the levee, Rummel said, "Well, that son of a bitch won't be testifying against me." At that point, according to Walker, he knew someone had been shot. Walker responded, "Let's get the hell out of here."

DeGeurin then asked Walker what everyone in the courtroom was wondering: Why would he get into the truck and leave with Rummel, knowing that Rummel had just taken a shot at someone inside Pepe's? Walker responded:

> WALKER: *To tell the truth, I did not think at all. I was pretty well scared, and I could not believe what he had done. I still had hopes that he had not done anything. I did not see anybody get hit....*
>
> DEGEURIN: *Why didn't you just say—"Let me out of here, you sorry SOB?" What was going through your mind during the drive back to Austin?*
>
> WALKER: *Well, the fact that I did not know Boyce Rummel very well. The fact that I did not know what he would do if I just got out of the vehicle and said let me out of here. He had $3,000 of my money, but at that time $3,000 was not all that important. I don't know—I have never been in that type of situation before. I was really indecisive. As I said, my foremost thought was getting back home and away.*

Jurors are instructed to use common sense when evaluating the evidence and determining the facts. Walker's explanation was neither reasonable nor rational. The jury might have believed him if he had testified that Rummel pointed the gun at him and forced him to get into the truck. But getting into the truck with a killer police would surely pursue makes no sense. Attributing the decision to fear or lack of thought was not believable. Also, later evidence would undermine Walker's testimony that he was afraid of Rummel.

Other evidence contradicted Walker's testimony. Ischy and Stotler, who testified to Rummel's irrational behavior, expressly said that Rummel intended to hire someone to kill Jimmy, not that he intended to kill Jimmy himself. Ischy even described a man he saw with Rummel on July 13 who he believed was the assassin, a description that matched Walker.

Also adverse to Walker was Rummel's testimony that one of the reasons he hired him stemmed from the time Walker accompanied Rummel and Stotler to retrieve Stotler's pickup truck. Walker testified that the incident never happened. He explained that Rummel and some "unidentified individual" needed Walker to give them a ride to pick up the truck. According to Walker, testimony that he acted as an armed enforcer was fabricated. He denied knowing Stotler.

After Walker testified, Pierce called Stotler as a rebuttal witness. He bolstered Rummel's testimony about Walker's participation in the pickup truck incident. According to Stotler, Walker offered him a pistol from the trunk of Walker's car, which contained several types of armaments. On cross-examination, DeGeurin pointed out that, like Rummel, Stotler was testifying under a plea agreement with the government, reducing his jail time. But the damage to Walker's credibility and his defense had been done.

Walker tried to explain away other incriminating facts. He told police after his arrest that he did not know Rummel by name because he only knew him as "BA" (badass). Walker further attributed his relocation from Austin to Ruidoso in December 1981 to a job. If he had said no more, the testimony of Walker's stepgrandfather, David Taylor, that Walker moved for work would have carried more weight. But Walker then testified that his reasons for leaving Texas included his connection to the shooting in the Valley.

Walker testified that he and his wife left Austin because he was "afraid that I might become involved in a crime that had been committed." He clarified that he was not worried about being charged but about being forced to be a witness against Rummel. "I was worried about it, yes. I did not want to become involved, and also I was partially in fear for my own life." According to Walker, he promised Rummel he would not say anything about the shooting.

> WALKER: *I feel guilty about what happened. I thought I might be implicated in the crime in some manner, and as I said, I thought I might be subpoenaed as a material witness. And I also thought there was a very good possibility that someone might try and kill me.*

Walker's explanation about fearing Rummel proved to be disingenuous. On cross-examination, Walker admitted that he visited Rummel at his home and spoke to him several times after the murders. Then, Edna Rummel, Boyce Rummel's wife, testified at trial that she spoke to Walker at a restaurant in Austin two to three days after her husband's arrest in November 1980. According to Edna, Rummel wanted her to ask Walker about the rifle. Pierce asked:

> PIERCE: *And tell us what conversation you had with Mr. Walker?*
> E. RUMMEL: *The conversation was over what had been done with the weapon.*
> PIERCE: *And what did you ask Mr. Walker?*

E. RUMMEL: If it had been disposed of, or what had been done with it.
PIERCE: And what was his response?
E. RUMMEL: He said that "It was in safekeeping, that a friend of his had it."

Edna provided more incriminating evidence against Walker. During their conversation, she and Rummel talked about David Ischy and his role in wearing a wire to obtain incriminating statements from Rummel about the murders. According to Edna, Walker said they should have done away with Ischy when he was originally arrested.

Pierce also asked Walker on cross-examination about his promise not to talk about the shooting:

WALKER: I promised that I would never mention that crime to anybody.
PIERCE: And it is a fact that you kept that promise until yesterday because up until yesterday, you'd never told any law enforcement authority be it Travis County where you were originally charged, the Hidalgo County, or the Federal Government about Rummel's involvement?

By his question and Walker's predictable answer, Pierce wanted the jury to know that Walker had never before accused Rummel of being the shooter. The jury might then conclude that the defense was fabricated for trial. DeGeurin strenuously objected that Pierce was commenting on Walker's prior silence in violation of his Fifth Amendment right to remain silent. Responding to DeGeurin's objection, Pierce noted that Walker had not remained silent but voluntarily told Travis County deputies that he did not know Rummel. He also pointed out that DeGeurin, on direct examination, brought up Walker's promise not to speak about Rummel's involvement. Cross-examination on the issue was fair game. The objection was overruled.

When Pierce finished his cross-examination of Walker, DeGeurin undoubtedly breathed a sigh of relief. Although inconsistencies in his testimony existed, Walker did not collapse under the pressure of Pierce's cross-examination. Despite its weaknesses, his testimony presented a viable explanation for the jury to consider. Rummel admitted his part in the effort to kill Jimmy, which resulted in the deaths of Charlotte and Kevin. The jury also heard how paranoid and crazy Rummel was acting. Now, they had testimony that Rummel impulsively picked up a rifle and shot into Pepe's. Walker and DeGeurin needed to turn the trial into Walker's word against Rummel's, which is precisely what they did. While evidentiary discrepancies existed, which Walker could not satisfactorily explain, he gave the jury an explanation they could rely on to acquit him. DeGeurin, thankful no more damage had been done, asked Walker no more questions. He rested the defense.

FINAL ARGUMENT

After six days of testimony, the end of the trial was near. All that remained were closing arguments, reading the legal instructions and jury deliberations. The burden on the government to prove guilt beyond a reasonable doubt gave the government an advantage in final arguments. Pierce and Murphy could present "opening" and "closing" final arguments before and after DeGeurin's final argument. Murphy began by reminding the jury to consider only the testimony and exhibits and by summarizing the law of conspiracy and the legal elements of a Section 241 offense.

Then, DeGeurin rose to make his final defense of Walker. As defense attorneys do in most criminal cases, he emphasized the heavy burden the government must satisfy to establish Walker's guilt beyond a reasonable doubt. Rummel's credibility remained the central issue. DeGeurin returned to the strong points he made during cross-examination. He told the jury that both Rummel and Stotler, who had testified that Walker provided him a gun from a trunk load of armaments, were convicted felons who "sold" their testimony to the government to minimize their time in jail. They were also Loop 360 Deal accomplices, and under Judge Garcia's instructions, their testimony must be considered by the jury with "great caution."

DeGeurin reminded the jury of the government's promise that if Rummel testified against Walker, he could save himself from the death penalty and limit his sentence on the Section 241 conspiracy to forty years instead of a life sentence. Additionally, Rummel could "wipe his slate clean" of other crimes and protect his family, giving him substantial motivation to implicate and testify against Walker.

DeGeurin stressed that while the plea agreement required that Rummel testify truthfully, the government, meaning Pierce, would decide if his testimony was "truthful." Then, DeGeurin took a calculated risk: "Did you notice how Boyce Rummel when I would ask him a question, he would look over to Pierce before he would answer?" DeGeurin was on solid ground in emphasizing that Rummel's testimony was critical to the government's case and that Rummel had a strong motivation for testifying that Walker was the shooter. But his question insinuating that Pierce might be influencing Rummel during the trial was highly improper.

Suggesting that opposing counsel is controlling a witness's answers as he testifies usually meets with a furious objection from the offended lawyer. Pierce sat quietly and said nothing. His calm response said more to the jury in defense of DeGeurin's implication than an objection. Pierce had not attempted to influence Rummel's testimony. The jury would have noticed if he had made gestures or facial expressions indicating to Rummel how he should respond. DeGeurin clarified that he was not suggesting that Pierce was telling Rummel to lie but that Rummel's glances indicated he was keenly aware that Pierce had to be satisfied with his answers. The plea agreement established that Pierce would determine if Rummel was telling the truth. That was the only point DeGeurin needed to make.

One of the most concerning issues for the government was the failure of the United States to prosecute the other men Rummel implicated in the murder conspiracy. DeGeurin fully exploited this weakness. He shrewdly suggested they were not charged because Pierce had doubts about the integrity of Rummel's testimony. And if Pierce had concerns, so should the jury. DeGeurin gave the jury a good reason to hesitate and find reasonable doubt of Walker's guilt.

Then, DeGeurin turned, if only briefly, to evidence that bolstered Walker's testimony that Rummel, not he, had killed Charlotte and Kevin. He recounted evidence that Rummel was berserk, ranting and raving about killing Jimmy. Someone so irrational could, in a desperate moment, act without thinking. Rummel, DeGeurin suggested, "could have picked up that gun and fired into the bar."

As his argument neared its close, DeGeurin redirected the jury to the crucial issue, "whether or not Mr. Walker fired that weapon [or] whether or not Mr. Boyce Rummel did." While emphasizing that point, he made a meager effort to express sympathy for the victims and their families. DeGeurin said, "We all agree that it is a tragic situation. My heart goes out to Charlotte Elliott—they do—I have children, but that is not the issue here." He was wrong—very wrong. The killing of Charlotte and Kevin was at the heart of the case; their deaths were both an emotional and a legal issue.

While the primary legal issue was whether Walker attempted to keep Jimmy from testifying, that offense paled compared to the deaths of two young and completely innocent people. Charlotte and Kevin died because of a senseless and despicable act. Everyone else, including the jury, understood and felt the heartbreaking loss. Though DeGeurin was facing the jury during his final argument, the jurors could not avoid glancing back at Joe and Gloria Elliott when DeGeurin said that Charlotte's murder was "not the issue."

Also, the indictment charged Walker with conspiracy to interfere with Jimmy's right to testify before a federal grand jury. That offense by itself carried a penalty of ten years in prison. The jury would be asked to decide if Walker's actions resulted in the deaths of Charlotte and Kevin. If so, the possible punishment he faced would be elevated to life in prison.

Also, DeGeurin's token reference to the murders did not remotely sound sincere. He would have been better served by fully acknowledging the immensity of the tragedy. He could have argued for Walker's acquittal without minimizing the heartbreaking loss to Joe and Gloria Elliott. The jury needed to know that Walker and DeGeurin comprehended the devastating and lasting impact of Rummel's act. In his testimony, Walker never mentioned Charlotte's and Kevin's names or said he felt terrible about what Rummel had done. Instead, he and DeGeurin came across as unsympathetic and uncaring. With that impression, the jury was left to decide the fate of the only person charged with the crime, Lloyd Chris Walker.

Communicating effectively with a jury is one of the most critical attributes a trial lawyer can possess. Though legally shrewd, good attorneys come across as humble, unpretentious and down-to-earth. They exude confidence and possess an uncanny ability to "connect" with a jury. Jurors can better understand what they are trying to say, unhampered by the legal jargon that some trial lawyers often use, and are more likely to see the case as the lawyer wants them to see it. The result is often a favorable verdict. During this author's career, a handful of lawyers demonstrated such an exceptional ability to talk to juries. Archie Carl Pierce was one of those lawyers.

Though still a young attorney in 1982, Pierce's final argument in Walker's case was masterful. Whatever seeds of hesitation and second thoughts DeGeurin had sown during his argument were soon uprooted. As did DeGeurin, Pierce went straight to the central issue in the case—credibility. Should the jury believe Rummel or Walker?

DeGeurin had zealously attacked the credibility of Rummel and Stotler, two of the government's most important witnesses. Pierce began by acknowledging that Rummel and Stotler were not saints. Both men were felons, Pierce noted. He pointed out that often, in criminal cases, the government must rely on other conspirators who have firsthand knowledge of the crime. He told the jury, "I would like to pick and choose the witnesses out of the community which you would believe, but they don't know anything about murder for hire." Pierce described the plea agreements with

Ischy, another felon, and Rummel as "good bargains," for which he made "no apologies." He explained, "Without those agreements, nobody would be brought to trial, and the crime would go unsolved."

Pierce did not ignore DeGeurin's argument that other people had not been prosecuted for the murders of Charlotte and Kevin. Pierce told the jury, "Ischy and Stotler are not on trial for this crime *yet*." For Pierce, prosecuting the shooter was the highest priority.

Then, Pierce methodically addressed every issue and all the relevant evidence supporting his belief that Rummel was telling the truth and Walker was not. Rummel's testimony, Pierce noted, did not stand alone; it was substantiated by physical evidence and other witnesses. He made a point that may have previously escaped the jury's notice. DeGeurin had had multiple opportunities to cross-examine Rummel about the crime itself. According to Pierce, "Mr. Rummel testified twice, and not on either one of those occasions did Mr. DeGeurin ask him one question or cross-examination about the facts of the case." From DeGeurin's standpoint, presenting Walker's version of the events at Pepe's was the rebuttal to Rummel's story. But once Pierce noted that DeGeurin allowed Rummel's testimony about events at Pepe's to go unchallenged, the jury would inevitably wonder why.

Pierce then turned to the believability of Walker's story and picked apart his version of the events in the Valley. During July 13, Walker said, Rummel was "ranting and raving" about Jimmy and his upcoming grand jury appearance. Then, later that day, they drove to Pepe's and by an extraordinary coincidence, ran into Jimmy "totally by accident." The implausibility of his story continued with Walker's testimony that he watched Rummel shoot into Pepe's, then drove back to Austin with him, "and it's life as usual until Mr. Rummel is arrested."

Pierce pointed out that Walker's testimony identifying Rummel, not he, as the killer was inconsistent with the taped, confidential conversation between Ischy and Rummel. On that tape and before he was arrested and made a plea agreement to implicate Walker, Rummel referred to a third person who had done the shooting. So, Pierce told the jury, "the testimony that Mr. Walker pulled the trigger was not fabricated *after* Mr. Rummel's arrest." The tape recording on which Rummel said, referring to a hit man, "He can't shoot worth a shit," provided strong evidence that someone other than Rummel was the shooter.

Pierce noted that, despite all his equivocation, Ischy confirmed that Rummel made calls to hire an assassin from Austin. And on July 13, Ischy saw the hit man, who matched Walker's description, with Rummel. Pierce emphasized, referring to Ischy, that "he does nothing whatsoever to support Walker's fabrication." Edna Rummel, who did not have a motive to lie, also provided incriminating evidence against Walker. She testified that Walker told her the murder weapon was in "safekeeping."

DeGeurin, no doubt feeling the body blows Pierce was delivering, stood up and objected to staunch the bleeding. DeGeurin said, "Your honor, I cannot argue anymore, and Mr. Pierce knows that, and I don't have a chance to answer him." What he said was true but not a valid objection. DeGeurin wanted the jury to believe that he would have something important to say if he could respond. Knowing there was no legal basis on which to rule, Judge Garcia simply acknowledged DeGeurin's statement, and Pierce resumed his argument.

In closing, Pierce reminded the jury about the victims: "The government awaits your verdict. Mr. and Mrs. Elliott await your verdict. The friends of Mr. Kevin Frase await your verdict." While Walker was on trial for intimidation of a witness, Pierce understood that the case was about far more than a failed drug deal or Jimmy's grand jury testimony; it was a murder case, a crime with innocent victims. His plea to the jury to remember Charlotte and Kevin contrasted sharply with DeGeurin's insensitive statement that the tragedy of Charlotte's and Kevin's deaths was "not the issue."

VERDICT

In the final instructions on the law governing deliberations, Judge Garcia advised the jurors that they must presume Walker was innocent unless and until the government proved his guilt beyond a reasonable doubt. On the all-important issue of the credibility of witnesses, Judge Garcia gave specific instructions:

> *In weighing the testimony of a witness, you consider his relationship to the government or the defendant; his interest, if any, in the outcome of the case; his manner of testifying; his opportunity to observe or acquire knowledge concerning the facts about which he testified; his candor, fairness and intelligence; and the extent to which he has been supported or contradicted by other credible evidence.*

The jury was instructed that the prior felony convictions of Rummel, Ischy and Stotler could be considered in weighing their credibility. Also, the testimony of accomplices with plea bargains, such as Rummel, Ischy and Stotler, must be "received with caution and weighed with great care." Walker's testimony would be weighed the same as that of any other witness. However, the jury could consider that, as the defendant, he had a "very keen personal interest" in the outcome of the case. The jury was further instructed that a defendant's conduct and statements made when confronted with a criminal charge can be considered in determining guilt or innocence. This instruction was relevant to the evidence that Walker fled to New Mexico after Rummel's arrest and then, after his arrest, denied knowing Rummel.

Just before jury deliberations, the two alternate jurors were excused. Only the original twelve would decide Walker's fate. While the jury was deliberating, DeGeurin called his boss, Percy Foreman, to update him. As the alternate jurors were leaving the courthouse, they were approached by the press and purportedly indicated they would have found Walker not guilty. DeGeurin told Foreman on the phone, "I just heard them say they would have voted not guilty. Things are looking good." Foreman replied, "You're an idiot. To me, things are looking bad. You just lost two 'not guilty' votes." Foreman hung up the phone.

The jury retired to the jury room with a copy of the indictment and a verdict form. Following the selection of a foreperson, deliberations began. Within a short time, the jury sent a note to Judge Garcia requesting a transcript of the testimony of Rummel and Walker. In 1980, court reporters recorded live testimony in shorthand on a stenograph during trials. Written transcripts were not available to juries during deliberations. Judge Garcia sent a note back to the jury telling them they must rely on their recollection of the evidence.

After three and a half hours of deliberation, the jury notified Judge Garcia it had reached a unanimous verdict. The attorneys were summoned back to court, and deputy marshals brought Walker in from his holding cell. Spectators slowly gathered in the courtroom gallery, including Joe and Gloria Elliott. After Judge Garcia took the bench, everyone anxiously waited as the court security officer departed to escort the jurors from the jury deliberation room. Even people who had not followed the trial regularly came to court to hear the verdict. No one spoke above a whisper.

Although Pierce and DeGeurin knew they had done all they could, the moments leading up to the reading of the verdict can be excruciating. As a matter of pride and reputation, attorneys care how a favorable or unfavorable verdict reflects on them. But for good lawyers like Pierce and DeGeurin, the primary concern is justice. Pierce wanted the jury to return a guilty verdict to punish Walker for his horrendous crime and for whatever peace of mind his conviction would bring to the Elliott and Frase families. DeGeurin passionately valued and sought to protect his client's constitutional rights—rights that silently protect everyone from wrongful prosecution. He wanted Walker to be acquitted because he genuinely believed a reasonable doubt existed as to his guilt.

Finally, the quiet of the courtroom was broken by the loud and distinctive knock of the court security officer. He opened the door and ordered, "All rise for the jury." Once the jurors were standing at their seats, Judge Garcia directed everyone to be seated. He asked the foreman if the jury had arrived at a verdict. The foreman responded that they had. The verdict form was given to the court security officer, who handed it to Judge Garcia. At the attorneys' tables, the hearts of Pierce, Murphy, DeGeurin and Walker began racing, though they tried to appear calm.

Judge Garcia read the verdict form: "We the Jury find the Defendant Lloyd Chris Walker, also known as Mike Walker, GUILTY as charged in the indictment." Despite the highs and lows of emotions, courtroom decorum mandated that everyone remain quiet; there was no outcry. To ensure that the verdict was unanimous, the clerk called each juror's name individually and asked them to confirm that "guilty" was their verdict. Each juror responded affirmatively. On June 17, 1982, slightly less than two years after Charlotte and Kevin were murdered, their killer was brought to justice.

Chapter 9

SENTENCING AND APPEAL

SENTENCING

In federal court, the judge, not the jury, imposes the punishment when a defendant pleads guilty or is found guilty after trial. A convicted defendant is rarely sentenced immediately. The United States Probation Office needs time to prepare a presentence investigation report (PSIR) for the judge. Through interviews with Walker and his father, the probation officer learned that Walker grew up in Lawton, Oklahoma, where he attended Jefferson Elementary School, Central Junior High School and Lawton High School through the eleventh grade. He was described as 5'10" and weighing approximately 150 pounds with blond hair, green eyes and a fair complexion. Walker had one sibling, an older sister, Merilynn.

In September 1969, at eighteen, Walker joined the United States Army and served in Vietnam. On September 1, 1970, he was honorably discharged and transferred to the United States Army Reserves, where he earned his GED. He tried a summer session of college but failed both classes.

According to the PSIR, Walker's criminal history was minimal. His father said Walker engaged in delinquent conduct at an early age "simply for excitement." In 1967, Walker accepted a friend's challenge to burglarize every café in Lawton. Nothing was stolen; he just wanted to break in. Mr. Walker believed that, after returning from Vietnam, his son was jailed for a lengthy time in Acapulco, Mexico. In 1975, he was convicted of burglary in Lawton and placed on probation. The PSIR reflected that Walker came from a "seemingly good family background, one in which no other family member has had difficulty with the law." Neither his parents nor his sister attended the trial.

Many lawyers consider the defendant's interview with the probation officer to be one of the most important interviews in his life. A defendant has the opportunity to make a positive impression on the probation officer whose report might, in turn, reflect a more hopeful outcome. Perhaps most importantly, the interview gives the offender the chance to express remorse for committing the crime. If the defendant is *sincerely* sorry, he has a much better chance of a lower sentence.

Based on DeGeurin's advice, Walker made no statement to the probation officer concerning the offense. He had denied his guilt at trial and intended to appeal the jury's verdict. DeGeurin did not want him to say something that could be used against him should there be another trial. Walker limited his responses to questions about simple background facts.

The interview did not help him. The probation officer found Walker's answers were "very short and to the point." Walker communicated with the probation officer but "showed little or no emotion." He sounded neither honest nor sincere. Walker's character would be judged solely by the evidence at trial and the jury's verdict that he was a hired assassin.

When DeGeurin read the PSIR, he realized it did not bode well. At sentencing, he told Judge Garcia that Walker had followed his advice during the interview and should not be penalized because of DeGeurin's guidance. Walker's failure to show emotion could not be attributed to DeGeurin's admonition not to talk about the case. At trial, Walker acknowledged he was present when Charlotte and Kevin were killed, and he drove off with the person he claimed was the shooter. Any reasonable person in those circumstances would feel something. Without admitting guilt, Walker could have expressed sorrow for the Elliott and Frase families, regret for his decision to leave Pepe's with Rummel or the wish that he had identified Rummel to law enforcement. He did nothing like that during his PSIR interview.

On August 19, 1982, Pierce, DeGeurin and Walker appeared before Judge Garcia for sentencing. Walker had done nothing to help himself in the PSIR interview. For Judge Garcia to see him as anything other than a cold-blooded killer, Walker's wife and his stepgrandfather, David Taylor, appeared and asked to speak to the court. Taylor told Judge Garcia he had known "Mike" since he was three. They were very close—more like father and son. Often, it is difficult for family members to accept that their loved one has committed a crime, especially one as heinous as this. Hoping for leniency, Taylor stated, "I know in my own heart that Mike is not guilty of this."

Walker's wife wrote a letter that Judge Garcia read before the sentencing. At the podium on August 19, she said:

> *I just come to speak for Mike and my family. I'd like for you to consider that letter and take it to your heart. What I said in this is what I feel and is honest, and it is as honest as I can be. Like I said, what is going happen today is very much pain to us all. And that more than anything, we have a little girl that is going to need Mike in her life.*

The time for a defendant in federal court to address the judge before sentencing is known as allocution. Some defendants take advantage of this important opportunity; others, for various reasons, choose to remain silent. Walker suffered from no shortage of words at trial and spoke again at sentencing, though only briefly. He stood before Judge Garcia and said:

> *I wish to thank your honor for his kindness that you extended to my wife and child throughout the trial process. And by that I mean providing the use of your chambers. I would like to express that I am very sorry for ever having become involved in this entire incident. And, more than anything, I am really sorry for the families and members of the deceased, and if there is anything I could do for them, I would. Other than that, I have one request to make of you, and that is that I be allowed to serve my sentence at Bastrop Federal Institute. The reason being I would like to be near my wife and child and near my grandparents.*

After two weeks of trial, having been convicted of causing the deaths of Charlotte and Kevin and now facing life imprisonment, Walker began by referencing Judge Garcia's simple, kind act of allowing his wife to sit in his office with their daughter during the trial. By that gesture, Judge Garcia showed Walker his humanity as a jurist. He demonstrated that he was not a cold-hearted bureaucrat and could be trusted with Walker's honesty. Walker should have realized that if Judge Garcia cared about his family, he would consider the impact of the sentence on everyone. But it remained imperative that Walker accept responsibility for his actions. Based on

DeGeurin's advice and Walker's intent to appeal, the opportunity to admit his wrongdoing and express sincere remorse was lost.

After the defendant is given the chance to speak, the attorneys can address the court regarding an appropriate sentence. DeGeurin used Rummel's implication of Ischy, Stotler and Burris in the murder conspiracy, and the government's reliance on Rummel's testimony, to his advantage. DeGeurin pointed out that Stotler and Burris received two to four years in jail for their part in the Loop 360 Deal, while Ischy got off scot-free. None of them had been prosecuted for the attempt to kill Jimmy. DeGeurin noted that Rummel, a convicted felon before the murder on the Rio Grande, escaped the death penalty and received forty years. Walker, DeGeurin argued, should receive less.

Not all DeGeurin's allocution was helpful. He reminded Judge Garcia that Walker had been charged with capital murder first in Travis County and then in Hidalgo County and was not convicted in either court. He asked Judge Garcia to consider that Walker "did bear that anxiety and did bear those trials, quietly defending himself honorably in a decent way, and had to go through it, and his family had to go through it." In a case where Walker was convicted of killing two innocent people, DeGeurin's argument portrayed him as a victim.

As for the deaths of Charlotte and Kevin, DeGeurin said:

> *It is stipulated—undisputed that there was no intent by anybody that those two individuals die....And, we know, all of us know that you cannot wipe it out whatever resulted—we all know that that was an accident.*

DeGeurin ended with a plea for mercy and leniency.

DeGeurin's reference to the killing of Charlotte and Kevin as an "accident" struck the wrong chord with Judge Garcia and Pierce. Pierce rose and said it was regrettable that Judge Garcia could not impose the death penalty. He emphasized that Walker was a "hired assassin" and that the shooting of Charlotte and Kevin was no accident. According to Pierce, "Walker carried out his duty and his job as a hired assassin in a cold-blooded manner." He asked Judge Garcia to impose the maximum sentence of life.

Although Pierce's argument should have been the last, DeGeurin requested the opportunity to respond. Perhaps knowing that the hammer was about to come down on Walker, Judge Garcia allowed him to do so. DeGeurin said the maximum penalty was for "someone who actually goes and kills somebody intentionally, knowingly and unlawfully under these circumstances." Again, he suggested that the deaths were "unintentional in a real human being sense." Judge Garcia took a recess to contemplate Walker's fate.

DeGeurin recalled thinking that Judge Garcia, who had been on the federal bench less than two years at the time of Walker's trial, did not possess "a lot of experience to gauge what's a horrible case and what's a less horrible case." DeGeurin thought this might be the "worst case he's seen." He was very wrong in that assessment. Many of the crimes Judge Garcia prosecuted as an assistant district attorney and presided over as a state district court judge were violent and tragic. Rape, robbery, sexual assault and murder cases were a staple of Judge Garcia's state court docket. As opposed to the "victimless crimes" that predominated in federal court, Judge Garcia now returned to the familiar setting of sentencing a defendant in a case with real and identifiable victims.

When he returned to the bench, Judge Garcia said, "Mr. Walker or Mr. DeGeurin, do you gentlemen know of any reason why the Court should not pass sentence at this time." Both responded, "No." Then, Judge Garcia pronounced:

> *It is the sentence of this Court that the defendant Lloyd Chris Walker is hereby committed to the custody of the Attorney General or his authorized representative for imprisonment for life.*

Relieved, Pierce hoped that the verdict and sentence gave Joe and Gloria some measure of peace. DeGeurin, disappointed, left the court to deliver the bad news to Percy Foreman.

From the author's years with Judge Garcia and personal experience of sentencing defendants as a magistrate judge, the author can provide insight into why Judge Garcia chose to sentence Walker to the maximum penalty. Walker told Judge Garcia, "And, more than anything, I am really sorry for the families and members of the deceased, and if there is anything I could do for them, I would." His one-sentence statement of regret was neither an apology nor an empathetic expression. Offering to do anything for the Elliott and Frase families was insulting.

Walker's poor attempt to express remorse also aggravated his situation. He said he was sorry for becoming involved in the "incident," but such regret was entirely selfish. Walker was sorry he had put himself and his family in this situation. He knew his stepgrandfather and his wife were undoubtedly suffering for the offense he committed. And he knew his daughter would grow up without her father. Walker never acknowledged responsibility for the deaths of Charlotte and Kevin. For a judge, the absence of some indication that the defendant is remorseful for his actions is difficult to overlook and often leads to a stricter sentence.

Most important in Judge Garcia's decision were the deaths of Charlotte and Kevin. The indescribable pain their families had suffered and would continue to suffer for the rest of their lives called for a sentence of life behind bars. Walker's wife told Judge Garcia that their daughter needed him in her life. Her husband's actions had deprived the Elliott and Frase families of having Charlotte and Kevin in their lives forever. DeGeurin's statement during his final argument that the killing of Charlotte and Kevin was "not the issue" and his insensitive comment that their deaths were an "accident" and "unintentional" served only to confirm Judge Garcia's sentencing decision.

In attempting to defend his client zealously, DeGeurin minimized the unspeakable and irreversible tragedy caused by Walker's actions. Both DeGeurin and Walker failed to recognize and express sincere regret for the unbearable and endless suffering the families of Charlotte and Kevin would endure. In a case where the lives of two completely innocent people were extinguished in the blink of an eye, DeGeurin's argument portrayed Walker as a victim. After a trial in which DeGeurin expertly and ardently defended Walker, his sentencing allocution did Walker no favors. Judges struggle daily with imposing appropriate sentences that balance the gravity of a crime and protect society with the hope that the defendant can be rehabilitated. Judge Garcia had no doubt that sentencing Walker to prison for the rest of his life was fully justified.

APPEAL

An appeal of Walker's conviction and sentence was inevitable. Facing life in prison, he had nothing to lose. In Walker's case, the primary avenue for challenging his conviction was a direct appeal to the United States Court of Appeals for the Fifth Circuit. DeGeurin continued to represent Walker for the appeal. In addition to Pierce, the government was represented by Assistant United States Attorney Sidney Powell, more recently noted as a member of Donald Trump's legal team who presented claims attacking the validity of the 2020 presidential election.

The most serious and potentially viable contention raised by DeGeurin on appeal concerned admission of the evidence of Walker's previous violent behavior. Legally, this evidence is referred to as "extrinsic acts," criminal acts besides the one for which a defendant is on trial. The "extrinsic acts" evidence against Walker came from Rummel, who testified that Walker bragged about prior violent behavior. Additionally, both Rummel and Stotler told the jury about the time Walker accompanied them as armed protection to retrieve Stotler's truck. The court of appeals held that Walker's boasts and actions were relevant to proving his knowledge and agreement to participate in the conspiracy to kill Jimmy. DeGeurin, the Fifth Circuit also noted, had "opened the door" on that issue when he cross-examined Rummel about his telephone call with Walker and asked whether Walker agreed to travel to the Valley to kill Jimmy.

Walker raised several other issues to overturn his conviction, which were rejected. He claimed that he could not be guilty of conspiring to "intimidate" a grand jury witness in the "free exercise or enjoyment of any right or privilege" because Jimmy was compelled to testify. The Fifth Circuit noted that few witnesses attend trials or appear before grand juries on a wholly voluntary basis; most are commanded by subpoena to appear. Although Jimmy was testifying because he had been held in contempt, it was still his decision. Walker did not challenge the imposition of the life sentence. His conviction was affirmed by the Fifth Circuit on July 15, 1983, almost three years to the day after he murdered Charlotte and Kevin. DeGeurin filed a petition to have his case reviewed by the United States Supreme Court, which was denied in 1984.

MOTION TO VACATE SENTENCE

Nine years later, Walker filed the second challenge to his conviction through a motion to vacate his sentence. Walker was represented by Austin attorney Stephen Orr, another experienced and well-respected criminal defense lawyer. Orr argued that Walker received ineffective assistance of counsel from DeGeurin because of a conflict of interest. The purported conflict arose from the third-party fee arrangement through which Walker's "friends" paid Foreman and DeGeurin to represent Walker. Such fee arrangements are not prohibited, but a problem arises when that arrangement becomes a factor in the attorney's advice and decision-making for his client. An actual conflict exists when defense counsel fails to pursue a plausible defense strategy or tactic because of his allegiance to the third party paying the defendant's fee.

In an affidavit submitted with his Section 2255 motion in 1993, Walker indicated that DeGeurin told him he had been hired by the same person who hired Rummel's attorney. Without providing a name, Walker stated that the person who hired the lawyers for him and Rummel was a "central figure" in the Loop 360 Deal. According to Walker, DeGeurin was adamant that the unnamed conspirator remain unidentified. Walker claimed that DeGeurin insisted on secrecy whenever the person's name was mentioned. Walker's wife supported her husband's claim by testifying that DeGeurin ripped a page from her address book containing the name of the brother of the unnamed conspirator.

Walker alleged that payment of the fee by the third party caused a conflict of interest that compromised DeGeurin's representation and Walker's defense. He stated that DeGeurin served the interests of the unnamed conspirator above Walker's. Though the alleged conflict of interest could compromise DeGeurin's entire representation of Walker, he claimed that DeGeurin's representation was deficient in only one respect. DeGeurin had clearly done an admirable job in zealously defending Walker at trial. Walker and Orr would be hard-pressed to prove that DeGeurin's representation during the entire trial was ineffective.

According to Walker, DeGeurin was hired to ensure that Walker would not cooperate with authorities and identify the unnamed conspirator. He contended that DeGeurin never sought a plea bargain with the government because of the conflict. He argued that DeGeurin did not initiate plea bargain negotiations with the government because DeGeurin "feared that [Walker] might disclose the identity and role of the conspirator" if Walker agreed to cooperate. By not seeking a plea agreement, which may have secured Walker a lighter sentence, DeGeurin, according to Walker, was protecting the person who paid his fee.

In August 1994, Orr took DeGeurin's deposition in support of Walker's Section 2255 motion. DeGeurin testified that he and Walker never talked about a plea bargain. DeGeurin also acknowledged that he and Pierce never discussed a plea agreement. According to DeGeurin, Walker always maintained that he was innocent and never asked DeGeurin to seek a favorable plea agreement. DeGeurin assumed Walker wanted a trial. Pierce testified by deposition that there was "no realistic possibility" of a plea bargain. According to Pierce, Rummel had already identified the unnamed conspirator to the government. So, Walker had no valuable information to trade for a lighter sentence. According to Pierce, the fact that Walker pulled the trigger and killed two innocent bystanders made it unlikely that a plea agreement could be reached.

In a report and recommendation to Judge Garcia in November 1997, a magistrate judge in Austin recommended rejection of Walker's conflict of interest claim. The judge concluded that Walker failed to prove that he wanted DeGeurin to engage in plea negotiations with Pierce or would have accepted a plea bargain if it had been offered. Judge Garcia accepted the reasoning and recommendation and, on November 25, 1997, denied Walker's motion to vacate his sentence. Walker again appealed. The Fifth Circuit Court of Appeals affirmed Judge Garcia's decision. The forty-six-year-old Walker had no more options to challenge his conviction and sentence. Though he became eligible for release after serving ten years of his life sentence, he would never be granted parole.

Chapter 10

THE AFTERMATH

PEPE'S ON THE RIVER

Remnants of Pepe's on the River.
Courtesy of John W. Primomo.

After many years of success, Pepe's fell on hard times. In 2010, two hurricanes and a tropical depression blew through south Texas, causing the Rio Grande to overflow its banks. Severe flooding inflicted extensive damage on the riverside bar—too much to repair. Pepe's closed. In 2014, new owners invested several hundred thousand dollars in the property, and Pepe's reopened. Then, on September 23, 2019, a fire engulfed and destroyed the easily combustible thatched-roof structure. Only a few palm trees surrounding the building survived. All that remains today of the once energetic and busy dance hall are the charred embers of the palapa scattered haphazardly on the concrete floor.

FAMILIES

Though tempered over time, the pain felt by the families of Charlotte and Kevin endures. Joe Elliott died Sunday, March 5, 2017. He was described as the epitome of a family patriarch, leaving an extensive family, including

Jane Vertrees Frase. *Courtesy of Keith Frase.*

his wife, Gloria; his remaining five children; and many grandchildren and great-grandchildren.

The heart of Jane Vertrees Frase was torn in two the night of July 13, 1980. Keith Frase said his mom was stoic and did not share her feelings. You knew the pain was there and could see it in her face, but no one understood the extent to which Kevin's death tortured her soul. The psychological and emotional damage never healed.

On March 14, 1983, four days before Kevin's thirty-first birthday and less than three years after he was killed, Jane Vertrees Frase took her life at the age of sixty, another victim of Walker and Rummel's senseless murders. Though her death became another "worst moment" in his life, Keith does not blame his mother for her decision, knowing the overwhelming grief she suffered. She is buried beside Kevin in Highland Memorial Park Cemetery in Weslaco, Texas.

Judge H.F. "Hippo" Garcia

After Walker's trial, Judge Garcia served another twenty years on the federal bench. He died on January 16, 2002, and is buried in the Texas State

Cemetery in Austin, alongside Stephen F. Austin, Congresswoman Barbara Jordan and a host of Texas governors. Aside from his many achievements, his tombstone bears the maxim he lived by: "To give dignity to a person is above all things." Hippo's closest friends, and they are many, treasure the honored memory of a man and judge so few were privileged to know.

John Christopher Burris and William Clayton "Sonny" Stotler

For his role in the Loop 360 Deal, Burris was convicted of conspiracy and possession of marijuana for distribution. He was sentenced in April 1980 to serve four years in the custody of the Bureau of Prisons (BOP). Burris was released on January 17, 1983. He was not charged in federal court with conspiring to kill Jimmy under Section 241 or in state court for the murders of Charlotte and Kevin.

Stotler, who drove the plane seats from the Valley to Austin, admitted that Rummel wanted him to locate Jimmy in the Valley and offer to pay him $10,000. He vehemently denied that he was "guilty of planning, [or] plotting in any way, shape or form" the death of Jimmy. For his part in the Loop 360 Deal and in consideration of his testimony at Walker's trial, Stotler was allowed to plead guilty to the lesser offense of hindering the apprehension of defendants engaged in the importation of marijuana. He was sentenced to two and a half years in prison in April 1981 and was released from BOP custody on January 23, 1984. Stotler was not charged in federal court under Section 241 for conspiring to kill Jimmy or in state court with the murders of Charlotte and Kevin. He died in 2019.

David Philip Ischy

Ischy, whose plea agreement led to the dismissal of his Loop 360 Deal charges and implication of Rummel in the murder plot, was a convicted felon before the Loop 360 Deal and continued to engage in drug trafficking after the Walker trial. Beginning in late April 1989, Ischy and other individuals agreed to import a large amount of cocaine from Mexico into Texas by plane. The scheme was remarkably like the plan used by the conspirators in the Loop 360 Deal. Ischy was caught with the cocaine and a loaded twelve-gauge shotgun.

Ischy was charged in federal court in Houston, pleaded guilty and was sentenced in March 1990 to eighteen years in prison for the drug offenses and five years for the weapons offense. As required by federal law, the five-year prison term for the gun charge was run consecutively to the eighteen-year drug sentence for a total of twenty-three years. No doubt recognizing that he faced a substantial term of imprisonment, Ischy planned to escape from custody while the cocaine and firearms charges were pending. His plan was discovered. In 1990, he was indicted in federal court for conspiracy to escape from federal prison. Again, he pleaded guilty. Another consecutive sentence of forty-six months was added to his other sentences for that crime. With both cases, Ischy would be serving 322 months in prison, almost twenty-seven years without the possibility of release on parole. In 1984, Congress passed the Sentencing Reform Act, which abolished parole for federal prisoners. While Rummel and even Walker, whose crimes were committed before 1984, would be eligible for parole, Ischy would not.

After time was credited toward his sentence for good conduct in prison, Ischy was released from BOP custody on December 6, 2012, having served twenty-three and a half continuous years in prison. Despite Rummel's testimony that Ischy was part of the murder conspiracy, Ischy, like Burris and Stotler, was never charged in federal court under Section 241 with conspiring to kill Jimmy or in state court for the deaths of Charlotte and Kevin. Yet, some might see his lengthy imprisonment for twenty-three and a half years, almost the same amount of time Rummel served for his Section 241 conviction, as poetic justice.

Boyce Wayne Rummel

In the months after the murders of Charlotte and Kevin, Rummel continued to use and sell drugs. His arrest in November 1980 on the Travis County capital murder charges put an end to his criminal life. That indictment was dismissed in December 1981. In June 1982, shortly after he testified at Walker's trial, the capital murder indictment against Rummel in Hidalgo County was dismissed. The Hidalgo County DA was satisfied he had faithfully fulfilled his part of the plea agreement. At that point, Rummel began the second year of his forty-year federal sentence under Section 241.

In June 1984, after Walker's conviction, Rummel filed a motion in federal court to modify his forty-year sentence. He had been sentenced in September

1981, long before Pierce and Judge Garcia knew whether or not he would fulfill his promise to testify against Walker. Rummel's request was not an attempt to set aside his conviction or receive a lower sentence. He wanted Judge Garcia to modify his sentence to give him a better chance at parole when the time came.

As his sentence stood, Rummel would be eligible for parole after serving one-third of his sentence, almost seventeen years. He hoped Judge Garcia would change his sentence to permit the Parole Commission to release Rummel at any time at its discretion. Satisfied with the extent of Rummel's cooperation, Pierce agreed to the sentence modification.

Judge Garcia did not. He acknowledged that Rummel's testimony was essential to Walker's conviction and life sentence. However, in his order denying Rummel's motion, Judge Garcia noted that Rummel was responsible for hiring Walker for the express purpose of shooting a potential grand jury witness, and he was present when the assassination attempt was made and two innocent bystanders were killed.

Judge Garcia stressed that Rummel could have been convicted of capital murder in state court and received a death sentence. By receiving a sentence of forty years rather than life, Rummel had already been given leniency for the Section 241 offense. By testifying against Walker, Rummel did no more than he was obligated to do under his plea agreement. Judge Garcia concluded that "to modify his sentence even lower would minimize the seriousness of his crimes and deride the memory of those whose lives he extinguished."

In 1990, Rummel received a mandatory parole review. He sought a positive recommendation from Pierce, which might help him when he became eligible for parole. By that time, Pierce had departed the United States Attorney's Office and was employed by an Austin law firm in private practice. Under U.S. attorney policy, he could not make a recommendation regarding Rummel's parole. He did, however, write a letter to the Parole Commission detailing the cooperation Rummel had provided in identifying and prosecuting Walker. Pierce noted that without Rummel, Walker would not have been convicted of the murders of Charlotte and Kevin. He also pointed out that Rummel, without obligation, assisted the government by testifying in federal prosecutions against three other individuals in 1984.

Rummel knew Pierce was not required to support his effort for parole. He appreciated the risk Pierce was taking, which could easily backfire if Rummel was released and reoffended. In a June 1989 letter, Rummel wrote back to Pierce. He told him that, over the years, he had learned to appreciate consistency in individuals. Rummel said he had no doubt where Pierce stood, judging right and wrong. He assured Pierce he would never again become involved in criminal activity.

Rummel also sought a good word from DEA special agent Dick Braziel, the case agent in the Loop 360 Deal, to obtain parole release. Indicative of the different mindsets and goals of prosecutors and law enforcement agents, Braziel emphatically said no. He believed that anyone who orchestrates the murder of another person should never get out of jail.

Rummel continued to serve his forty-year sentence and was released from the Bureau of Prisons on January 9, 2004, after serving twenty-four years. Rewarding the faith Pierce placed in his star witness, Rummel never again was arrested, prosecuted or convicted of any crime in state or federal court. He was true to his word.

Lloyd Chris Walker

Only a criminal psychologist can offer an expert opinion on the possible reasons Walker shot and killed Charlotte and Kevin. Based on the author's years of legal experience, Rummel's offer to pay Walker $10,000 played a part in his decision-making process but was not the fundamental reason for his willingness to kill. A person's nature and character determine the value he places on a human life. Aside from his boasts, he had no prior violent history. He would commit no violence during the many years he spent in federal prison, and psychological testing in prison demonstrated no mental abnormalities.

While causes of criminal behavior are varied, traumatic or abusive childhoods often contribute to criminal behavior as an adult. Walker's presentence investigation report (PSIR) reflects that Walker's father had nothing good to say about his son. His failure to appear at Walker's trial strongly indicates the absence of any ongoing father-son relationship. Walker's father died on November 8, 1983, while his son was in federal prison. None of Walker's prison records reflect any feelings, positive or negative, about the loss of his father. The circumstances surrounding his death raise questions about the Walker family and the household in which Walker was raised.

On November 8, 1983, Walker's sister, Merilynn, shot and killed their father in Lawton and then kidnapped their mother. Merilynn was captured, and Walker's mother was unharmed. In February 1992, many years later, Merilynn was charged with first-degree murder. After various court proceedings determined that she was mentally competent and sane at the time of the offense, she pleaded guilty to second-degree murder and was sentenced to twenty years in the Oklahoma Department of Corrections. She was discharged from custody on February 22, 2000. The motives for her crime are unknown.

After sentencing in August 1982, Walker was transferred to the custody of the Bureau of Prisons and was assigned prisoner number 09795-079. A month after sentencing, Walker was designated to Federal Correctional Institution (FCI) Bastrop, a low-security institution forty-five minutes from Austin, where his wife and child lived. However, the severity of his offense resulted in a High/MAX classification, requiring confinement in a higher-security facility. In December 1982, Walker was transferred to United States Penitentiary (USP) Terre Haute in Indiana.

For the most part, Walker was considered an average inmate by prison staff, doing no more than was required to serve his time. Throughout his imprisonment, he repeatedly refused to comply with prison rules and regulations, resulting in the imposition of disciplinary sanctions. Walker's infractions were typically minor offenses such as disrespect, refusal to obey an order and lack of tidiness. By far, the majority of Walker's institutional violations centered on his possession and use of drugs.

The drugs might be found in his cell or on his person, or a positive urine test might establish he had ingested a controlled substance. Walker rarely challenged the charges; he seemed indifferent. Although he was found in possession of cocaine on a handful of occasions, his drug of choice was marijuana. Drug treatment was offered to him and recommended, but Walker refused. He denied that he had a drug problem. Possession or use of narcotics can—and did, in Walker's situation—result in the loss of commissary, telephone and visitation privileges. Placement in administrative segregation or loss of single-cell privilege could also be imposed.

For Walker, his repeated drug possession became a joke. In October 1990, he attributed a positive test for cocaine to a "green pill," which he found inside an administrative segregation cell and ingested. In May 1991, Walker gave another tongue-in-cheek excuse for a positive marijuana test. He told the disciplinary hearing officer, "I haven't smoked marijuana in three and a half months except for the joint I shared with a friend about a week and a half before the test." Between 1983 and 1991, Walker was found guilty of possessing narcotics fourteen times.

Walker's willingness to continually violate prison drug policies is curious, given that his actions did have adverse consequences. He certainly knew the odds of being caught were high. Maybe he could conceal the drugs—though, apparently, he was not very adept at it—but his use would inevitably be discovered when he was tested. Also, in prison, the privileges of telephone use, visitation and access to the commissary, which could be taken away as punishment, are valuable. And few prisoners want isolated confinement. Walker's aberrant behavior was especially destructive considering its impact on his parole release. His repeated disciplinary infractions and refusal to participate in available programs for drug treatment significantly hurt his release chances.

Walker received his initial parole hearing in 1998, sixteen years after being sentenced. A parole examiner recommended denying parole in light of his original offense and numerous prison disciplinary infractions. Represented by Stephen Orr, his Section 2255 lawyer, Walker sought review by a Parole Commission panel. He claimed that his offense was improperly considered a contract murder. Walker's continued denial of guilt and his assertion of defenses rejected at trial only hurt his chances of being released.

The panel reviewed Walker's PSIR, which reflected that the jury found he had been hired for $10,000 to commit a murder. The panel determined that Parole Commission regulations required that Walker be denied parole in the absence of compelling circumstances in mitigation, which did not exist in his case. Parole was denied, and he was "continue[d] to expiration." Parole was again refused in 2000.

A new century brought no change in Walker's attitude. His repeated possession of drugs continued to result in the suspension of privileges and administrative segregation. Once, Walker was cited for having an unsanitary and untidy cell. Reflecting his lack of motivation for release, he told the disciplinary hearing officer he had "19 calendar years to do" and did not want anyone telling him what to do.

Walker was not considered for parole again until March 2012. The parole examiner noted that since his last appearance before a parole panel in 2000, Walker had incurred fourteen drug-related disciplinary infractions and chosen not to participate in drug treatment programs. At the hearing, Walker, now sixty-one, said he was sorry for the acts he committed, referring to the July 1980 murders of Charlotte and Kevin. The parole examiner did not believe he was genuinely remorseful. Due to Walker's continued disciplinary infractions and his commission of a contract murder, the examiner recommended that parole again be denied. In April, Walker's request for parole was refused.

Walker's next parole hearing was set for March 2014. As for the killing of Charlotte and Kevin, Walker, returning to his trial defense from thirty-two years before, insisted that he was not an assassin. He claimed his offense was not a contract murder but a drug deal. Parole was again denied. He would not be considered for release again.

As Walker got older, medical records replaced disciplinary records in his prison file. In October 2014, cancer was found in his left lung, which was partially removed. The tumor was small, and at that time, doctors felt that his chances of being cured were high. CT scans of his chest and abdomen in March 2015 were normal. He remained active into 2015, telling one physician he felt more like someone twenty-five years old rather than his age of sixty-four.

Suddenly, in late summer 2015, Walker's health changed dramatically. He began having significant shortness of breath, decreased exercise tolerance and dark stools. For several weeks, severe abdominal pain accompanied the other symptoms. Finally, in October, when he could no longer tolerate the pain, he sought medical help. The doctor asked Walker why he had waited so long. His odd response: "The long line is embarrassing when you wait to see a doctor."

On October 15, 2015, Walker was admitted to a local hospital. He was profoundly anemic and needed to be resuscitated and transfused. Evaluation showed a bowel perforation that required surgery. The surgeon diagnosed Walker with metastatic lung adenocarcinoma. A positron emission tomography (PET) scan suggested another mass in his right lower quadrant. The prison chaplain notified Walker's sister.

Walker remained hospitalized. By November 25, his condition had worsened, and he signed a DNR (do not resuscitate) order. Walker died at 6:18 a.m. on November 30, 2015, at the age of sixty-four. Charlotte would have been fifty-four years old then; Kevin, sixty-three. Walker had served thirty-three and a half years, more than half of his life, in federal prison for their murders. The life sentence Judge Garcia imposed had been satisfied.

Walker's body was removed to Lawton, Oklahoma, for burial. His obituary indicates that his wife and daughter survived him and lived in Duluth, Minnesota. His stepgrandfather, David S. Taylor, who stood by Walker and did not believe in his heart that Walker had committed such a heinous crime, also outlived him.

WALKER'S CONVICTION BROUGHT A semblance of closure to the need for legal justice, though it did little to assuage the emotional pain and suffering of the families of Charlotte and Kevin. Moral justice will never be satisfied. Other than his pitiful wish at sentencing to do what he could for the families, Walker offered them nothing. He never reached out, not once, to let them know he was sorry—to tell them that he would take it back if he could.

Walker's parole records reflect his mindset never changed, even after years in prison. At sixty-one, he told the parole examiner he was sorry for his crime, hoping his apology would help him get parole. He was not genuinely contrite. Walker continued to deny being involved in a contract killing and even denied being the killer. Confronting death often has the sobering effect of forcing a person to drop pretenses and make peace with those he has harmed. As the end approached in 2015, Walker had a final opportunity to contact the Elliott and Frase families, admit he killed Charlotte and Kevin and express sorrow for his actions. He did nothing.

In July 1980, Rummel faced no more than ten years in jail if he was convicted of his part in the Loop 360 Deal. In all likelihood, with parole, he would have served no more than three or four years. Yet, he was willing to kill rather than accept responsibility for his drug dealing. His criminally selfish decision caused the deaths of two young people who had no involvement with the Loop 360 Deal and unimaginable pain to their families.

Like Walker, Rummel, too, owes more than a debt to society. He served twenty-four years of his forty-year sentence and never violated parole. As he promised Pierce, he did not reengage in criminal behavior. Obeying the law, though, is no more than is required of any person. Morally, Rummel has not atoned for taking the lives of Charlotte and Kevin. Whether he can make amends for what he did is a matter only he and the families of Charlotte and Kevin can determine. Time and opportunity will soon pass forever.

Despite the passage of years, the loss to the Elliott and Frase families remains very real today. Perhaps no day goes by without a sad thought or reminder. Though life comes with no guarantees, the precious lives of Charlotte and Kevin ended far too soon. Their deaths cannot be rationalized. Neither of them knew Rummel, Walker or Jimmy. They had no reason to worry about drug traffickers, federal witnesses or assassins. They were simply young people enjoying life. What Rummel and Walker took cannot be measured. Time was taken from Charlotte and Kevin and their families without warning. Charlotte and Kevin were deprived of years filled with laughter, joy, love, successes and disappointments, good times and bad times—they were robbed of life. Had they lived, Charlotte and Kevin might be parents and grandparents by now, with families of their own. Through all the facts about the marijuana conspiracy, Jimmy's arrest, the attempt to silence him, the murder conspiracy, the court cases against Rummel and the prosecution of Walker, this book has always been about remembering Charlotte and Kevin.

NOTES

Chapter 1

1. Maril, *Patrolling Chaos*, 83.
2. Mayo Clinic, "Cerebral Palsy."
3. The Old Farmer's Almanac, "Weather History for McAllen, TX."
4. Words cannot possibly convey the painful thoughts and feelings endured by the parents of a murdered child. A dramatic portrayal of a real-life child murder gives some sense of the devastating pain and suffering. *Little Boy Blue* (2017) is a true crime drama about the murder of eleven-year-old Rhys Jones, who was shot and killed on August 22, 2007, in Liverpool, England, as he walked home from football practice.

Chapter 2

5. United States Drug Enforcement Administration, "1975–1980," 47.
6. United States Drug Enforcement Administration, "The DEA Years," 34.
7. Elliott, "1980s Marijuana Smugglers."
8. Ryan, *Jackpot*, vii.
9. Elliott, "1980s Marijuana Smugglers."
10. Northcott, "All Roads"; University of Texas at Austin Office of Institutional Studies, *Statistical Handbook*, 1.
11. Jackson, *One Ranger Returns*, 123–31.

Chapter 3

12. Statements herein that Ischy, Stotler and Burris plotted to kill Jimmy are derived solely from the testimony of Rummel at Walker's trial. Ischy and Stotler vehemently denied that they agreed to or participated in the plan. Burris did not testify.

Chapter 4

13. Safwat, "Section 241," 625–26.

Chapter 5

14. Wikipedia, "Percy Foreman."

Chapter 6

15. Wright & Greenhill PC, "Archie Carl Pierce."
16. Wikipedia, "Jamiel Chagra."
17. Draper, "Great Defenders."
18. Law Offices of Foreman, DeGeurin & DeGeurin, "Mike DeGeurin."
19. Draper, "Great Defenders"
20. Law Offices of Foreman, DeGeurin & DeGeurin, "Mike DeGeurin."
21. LinkedIn, "Mike DeGeurin."
22. Carabin, *One-of-a-Kind Judge*, 27–28.
23. Ibid.
24. Ibid.

Chapter 7

25. Darrin, "Fingerprint Identification."
26. Law Offices of Foreman, DeGeurin & DeGeurin, "The Legacy of Percy Foreman."

BIBLIOGRAPHY

Carabin, Joan Cook. *One-of-a-Kind Judge: The Honorable Hippo Garcia*. Bloomington, Indiana: LifeRich Publishing, 2014.

Darrin. "The History and Evolution of Fingerprint Identification." North American Investigations, November 26, 2013. https://pvteyes.com/history-evolution-fingerprint-identification/.

Draper, Robert. "The Great Defenders." *Texas Monthly*, January 1994. https://www.texasmonthly.com/news-politics/the-great-defenders/.

Elliott, Steve. "1980s Marijuana Smugglers Recall the Glory Days." Toke of the Town, June 27, 2011, https://www.tokeofthetown.com/2011/06/1980s_marijuana_smuggler_recalls_the_glory_days.php/.

Jackson, H. Joaquin, with James L. Haley. *One Ranger Returns*. Austin: University of Texas Press, 2008.

Law Offices of Foreman, DeGeurin & DeGeurin. "The Legacy of Percy Foreman." Accessed June 19, 2022. https://foremandegeurin.com/legacy.html.

———. "Mike DeGeurin." Accessed October 18, 2022. https://www.foremandegeurin.com/mike.html

LinkedIn. "Mike DeGeurin." Accessed October 18, 2022. https://www.linkedin.com/in/mike-degeurin-7a29006.

Maril, Robert Lee. *Patrolling Chaos: The U.S. Border Patrol in Deep South Texas*. Lubbock: Texas Tech University Press, 2004.

Mayo Clinic. "Cerebral Palsy." Accessed April 24, 2020. https://www.mayoclinic.org/diseases-conditions/cerebral-palsy/symptoms-causes/syc-20353999.

Northcott, Kaye. "All Roads Lead from Roma." *Texas Monthly*, April 1977, https://www.texasmonthly.com/articles/all-road-lead-from-roma/.

The Old Farmer's Almanac. "Weather History for McAllen, TX." July 13, 1980. https://www.almanac.com/weather/history/TX/McAllen/1980-07-13.

Ryan, Jason. *Jackpot: High Times, High Seas, and the Sting That Launched the War on Drugs*. Guilford, CT: Lyons Press, 2012.

Safwat, Adam G. "Section 241 and the First Amendment: Avoiding a False Conflict Through Proper *Mens Rea* Analysis." *Duke Law Journal* 43, no. 3 (December 1993): 625–70. https://scholarship.law.duke.edu/cgi/viewcontent.cgi?article=3239&context=dlj.

United States Drug Enforcement Administration. "The DEA Years." In *DEA History in Depth*. Accessed April 8, 2020. https://www.dea.gov/sites/default/files/2018-07/1970-1975%20p%2030-39.pdf.

———. "1975–1980." In *DEA History in Depth*. Accessed April 8, 2020. https://www.dea.gov/sites/default/files/2018-07/1975-1980%20p%2039-49.pdf.

The University of Texas at Austin Office of Institutional Studies. *Statistical Handbook*. Accessed May 25, 2020. https://utexas.app.box.com/v/SHB80-81Complete.

Wikipedia. "Jamiel Chagra." Accessed November 9, 2021. https://en.wikipedia.org/wiki/Jamiel_Chagra.

———. "Percy Foreman." Accessed March 28, 2022. https://en.wikipedia.org/wiki/Percy_Foreman.

Wright & Greenhill PC. Archie Carl Pierce. https://www.wrightgreenhill.com/attorney/archie-c-pierce/ Accessed October 18, 2022.

ABOUT THE AUTHOR

John W. Primomo served twenty-nine years as a United States magistrate judge for the Western District of Texas in San Antonio. He previously authored two books: *The Appomattox Generals: The Parallel Lives of Joshua L. Chamberlain, USA, and John B. Gordon, CSA, Commanders at the Surrender Ceremony of April 12, 1865* (2013) and *Architect of Death at Auschwitz: A Biography of Rudolf Höss* (2020). For more than thirty years, he has volunteered with Camp Discovery, a summer camp in south Texas for children with cancer. He is also the president of the nonprofit corporation that operates Camp Discovery and several other camps for children with life-threatening illnesses and their families throughout the year.

Visit us at
www.historypress.com
··